CASUAL COSPLAY

CASUAL COSPLAY

Character-Inspired Fashion
You Can Wear Anywhere

KRYSTAL EVERDEEN

TILLER PRESS

NEW YORK   LONDON   TORONTO   SYDNEY   NEW DELHI

TILLER PRESS

An Imprint of Simon & Schuster, Inc.
1230 Avenue of the Americas
New York, NY 10020

First Tiller Press trade paperback edition June 2021

For information about special discounts for bulk purchases, please contact Simon & Schuster Special Sales at 1-866-506-1949 or business@simonandschuster.com.

The Simon & Schuster Speakers Bureau can bring authors to your live event. For more information or to book an event, contact the Simon & Schuster Speakers Bureau at 1-866-248-3049 or visit our website at www.simonspeakers.com.

Interior design by Matt Ryan

Manufactured in the United States of America

1   3   5   7   9   10   8   6   4   2

Library of Congress Cataloging-in-Publication Data has been applied for.

ISBN 978-1-9821-5059-4
ISBN 978-1-9821-5060-0 (ebook)

To those who never stop
believing in magic

CONTENTS

INTRODUCTION

We all had a blast playing dress up when we were little—but who said we ever had to stop? Sure, maybe we can't go full costume anywhere but a comic book convention or a Halloween party, but that doesn't mean we can't add some superhero or princess vibes to our everyday look. Casual cosplay is taking regular clothes that you already have in your wardrobe and styling them in a way that resembles what a certain character wears. It's distinct from full cosplay, which often incorporates wigs, colored contact lenses, extreme makeup, and meticulously assembled outfits to embody a character as accurately as possible. In casual cosplay, the styling choices are much more subtle. The average person sees a normal look, but those familiar with the character you're cosplaying can make the connection.

So how does one put together a casual cosplay? I'll share my tips and tricks for creating fun outfits inspired by your favorite characters for little or no money. Let's begin!

My name is Krystal Everdeen, and I'm a style blogger and YouTuber—and, as you can probably guess, a big fan of all things Disney, Harry Potter, Star Wars, and more. I began sharing casual cosplays of my favorite Disney characters on my Instagram account for my frequent trips to Disneyland. Since Disneyland doesn't allow anyone over the age of fourteen to wear costumes to the park, us Disney-lovers participate in a specific form of casual cosplay called "Disneybounding." The term *Disneybound* was coined by blogger Leslie Kay in 2011. In anticipation of a trip to Disney World, Kay began sharing different outfit ideas she'd Photoshopped together to resemble Disney characters. The images inspired countless Disney fans, who formed a community to share their own ideas and strategies. It's now a common practice for Disney-lovers to dress up at the parks in casual cosplay without violating the costume rule.

After posting a number of notable Disneybounds on my page, I started to branch out to other fandoms, such as Star Wars, Harry Potter, and more. As these posts gained traction, I began uploading casual cosplay and Disneybounding videos to my YouTube channel. In each video, I showed four different ways to dress as the same character. The great thing about casual cosplay is that there are no rules! You can always add your own twist or change the look over time. I've always loved clothes, but I'd never had so much fun with fashion until I discovered Disneybounding and casual cosplay. What started out as a fun little hobby has become one of my true passions—and a dream career.

GETTING STARTED

My favorite thing about casual cosplay is that you can use what you already own. When I first started Disneybounding, I put together my outfits with some basics I had in my closet. My very first casual cosplay was Princess Leia from Star Wars. The outfit consisted of a plain white turtleneck sweater, a white maxi skirt, a silver belt, and white sneakers. I put my hair up in two buns, and presto! That outfit cost me zero dollars. Shortly thereafter, I dressed as Mickey Mouse, again using what I already owned: a black long-sleeved top, a red hoop skirt, a pair of plain black shoes, and a pair of Mickey ears I had snagged on a previous trip to Disneyland.

I always try to use what I already have, because who wants to spend more money than necessary? There are, however, times when I need a specific color, article of clothing, or accessory that I don't have handy. Even then, I try my best to be as thrifty as possible; I do most of my casual cosplay shopping at secondhand shops and thrift stores. Luckily, these stores usually group their items of clothing by type and color. If I'm looking for a purple short-sleeved shirt for an Ariel-inspired look, I know exactly where to go because of the way the store is arranged.

Thrift stores' other appeal is low prices. Typically, anything you buy from a secondhand store will be significantly cheaper than the same item would be at a retail store, or even online. Contrary to popular belief, the clothing at thrift stores is usually either lightly worn or brand-new. I've found many stunning pieces during my thrifting adventures, and I highly recommend trying that route before purchasing what you're looking for from a popular fashion brand, especially if the piece is for a single occasion. Plus, if you need to alter the clothing in some way to fit the character better, you won't hesitate to do so.

Of course, there are times when I can't find what I'm looking for at a thrift store. For example, I was recently planning a Jane Porter Disneybound from the movie *Tarzan*. I scoured my local thrift stores for days, finding a hat and scarf that fit the character perfectly, but I couldn't locate the right yellow dress. In the end, I decided to look online. I found a dress on Amazon for thirty dollars, which is more than I would usually spend on a single piece, but since it was a plain dress that I could use for other Disneybounds and casual cosplays, it was worth it.

If you have a larger budget for your outfits, even better! Just don't feel that you have to spend big—the community is all about fun, not fancy.

Since I got my start with Disney-inspired outfits, I'll open this guide with Disneybounds, including everyone's favorite princesses and villains, as well as some lesser-known characters. For those whose allegiances lie elsewhere, never fear—we'll cover everything from Star Wars to Marvel, DC, and even your favorite TV cartoon characters. Let's go!

CHAPTER 1

DISNEYBOUND

Mickey & Friends

The most iconic group of Disney characters is Mickey Mouse and his friends. Although they vary greatly in appearance, they all sport recognizable color schemes, which are the key to successfully executing this category of cosplay. For example, there are countless ways to dress like Mickey, given his long film history, but his classic outfit is red shorts, yellow shoes, and white gloves. With those visual cues, this cosplay is hard to miss.

MICKEY MOUSE

To put together a casual cosplay or Disneybound for Mickey Mouse, make sure that your clothing coordinates with this color scheme, and in the proper places: black top, red bottom, and yellow shoes—and don't forget the most important accessory: a pair of Mickey ears. They're sold in a variety of colors, textures, and patterns. Although they were originally exclusive to Disney theme parks, you can now purchase them at your local Disney store or online. No matter how simple or complex your Mickey Mouse–inspired look may be, the ears will always be the cherry on top!

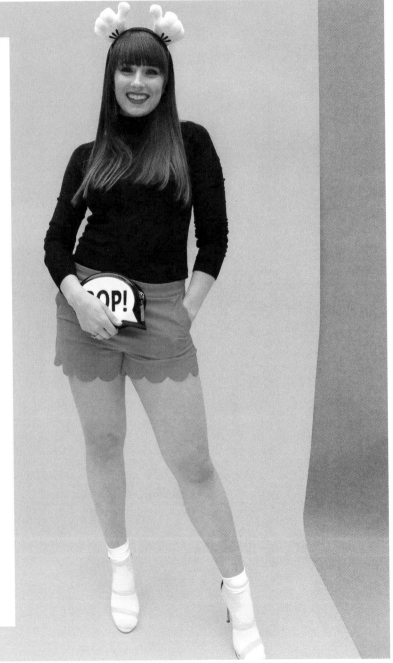

Now, despite the fact that Mickey Mouse is male, women dress as him without raising any eyebrows. As with any casual cosplay, gender doesn't matter; in fact, experimentation is the name of the game! The Mickey cosplays I'm going to share lean more toward the feminine side, but the color-coordination concept applies to all styles.

For the first outfit, Disney fan Tara Lau (@taradlau on Instagram) (left) styled a black long-sleeved turtleneck with a pair of red shorts and accessorized with a fun Pop handbag and a headband in the shape of Mickey's gloves.

If you don't own a Mickey-glove headband, switch it out for a classic Mickey ear headband. On her feet, Tara wore white socks with yellow heels. If you're planning on wearing this outfit to the parks or would prefer to wear comfortable shoes, however, you can substitute flats for the heels, or wear yellow socks that peep out of your shoes or sneakers. So as long as you have a simple black top and a red bottom in your wardrobe, you're halfway there.

Again, there are countless ways to style an outfit based on a character. If you're looking for a more masculine take, a black T-shirt worn with red shorts or pants and yellow shoes or socks is all you need to channel Mickey for the day.

While I personally believe that a pair of Mickey ears is essential to the look, there may be an occasion when the ears wouldn't be appropriate. In that case, consider the subtler approach of Instagrammer Tatum Blinn (@disneytate). Tatum's outfit consists of an all-black polka-dotted top from Forever 21, a red denim skirt from American Eagle Outfitters, a black belt from Nordstrom, pastel yellow sandals from Walmart, and a black hat from Brixton. A hat is a fun variation on the ears, and one true fans will appreciate.

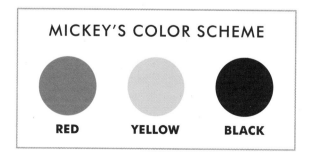

MICKEY'S COLOR SCHEME

RED   **YELLOW**   **BLACK**

MINNIE MOUSE

Like Mickey, Minnie Mouse has a number of iconic outfits you can choose from for your casual cosplay. However, the most recognizable Minnie look is her red polka-dotted dress, red polka-dotted bow, and yellow shoes. If you already own a red dress with white polka dots, you're in luck! All you need is a bow. And when dressing as Minnie, an alternative to mouse ears is styling your hair in two small buns on top of your head. Even people who don't recognize Minnie will still see a super-cute outfit—the beauty of casual cosplay!

If you don't already own a red polka-dotted dress, you can pair a black top with a red polka-dotted skirt.

The polka dots are Minnie's signature, but another classic Minnie look is her blue-and-white polka-dotted dress, which she accessorizes with a little red hat with a flower and yellow heels. Similar to the red polka-dotted outfit, you can create a spot-on casual cosplay if you already own a blue-and-white polka-dotted dress. I was lucky enough to find the perfect dress (right) for this outfit at a thrift store. It looks vintage, but it's actually from the brand Grace Karin and is conveniently sold on Amazon for less than forty dollars. I styled it with a red beret from the pop-culture store BoxLunch, a pair of white lace gloves from Amazon, and a pair of yellow heels I also thrifted.

As you may have noticed, this second Minnie Mouse look is a bit dressier than the first. It's perfect for an event where you might want to dress formally but still wear a casual cosplay. Those of us in the Disney community often wear these elegant looks for an occasion called Dapper Day, a semiannual gathering started by stylish Disney fans and inspired by the fashion of the mid-1950s, when Disneyland first opened. Although not officially endorsed by Disney, Dapper Day has become an incredibly popular event, when the crowds at Disneyland are noticeably dressier and more festive. One Dapper Day is held in the spring and another in the fall, so if you ever need an excuse to fancy up your Disney cosplay, mark your calendar!

Minnie Mouse's Classic Look

- Blue-and-white polka-dotted dress
- Red hat with a flower
- Yellow heels

DONALD DUCK

Another popular friend of Mickey's is Donald Duck. Donald's color scheme is blue, white, and yellow. He's often seen wearing a blue sailor top with white trim and a red bow, along with a matching blue beret. Since he doesn't wear pants, Disneybounds and casual cosplays of the character usually incorporate white bottoms to match his feathers and yellow shoes to match his feet.

For my Donald Duck–inspired outfit, I matched a solid blue knit sweater with a white circle skirt and added a petticoat underneath the skirt to give a feathery look (left). I then accessorized with yellow crew socks, white booties, and a blue beret.

If you want to re-create this look but with more comfortable shoes, a pair of yellow sneakers would still look great. To complete the cosplay, I incorporated my Donald Duck backpack, a Loungefly x Disney design that's available in a number of retail and online stores. Bags, purses, and backpacks can make a huge difference when it comes to styling these outfits, so if you have any that would go well with your look, don't be afraid to use them!

A blue dress with a red belt and yellow heels would also serve as an adorable Donald Duck cosplay.

Disney enthusiast Erica Lau (@ericarlau on Instagram) (right) put together this Donald outfit using a blue-and-white checkered two-piece set from SHEIN, adding that essential yellow detail with a cardigan draped around her shoulders.

This outfit is less on the nose than the others, but as long as you stick to the general color scheme of a character, you can be as creative as you'd like. If you don't own a blue knit sweater or a blue-and-white checkered set, or are looking to wear something other than a dress or a skirt, a quick and easy way to channel Donald Duck is with a blue tank top, white shorts, a blue hair accessory, and yellow shoes or socks. Men often wear blue button-downs or T-shirts with white jeans and yellow shoes. Occasionally—especially on Dapper Day—I'll also see men wear red bow ties with their Donald outfits, and sometimes even yellow suspenders. These can serve as a nod to Donald's sailor top and beret.

DONALD DUCK'S SIGNATURE COLOR SCHEME

BLUE   WHITE   YELLOW

DAISY DUCK

Another fashionable member of the Clubhouse is Daisy Duck, Donald's girlfriend. Daisy's most popular outfit consists of a **lilac puff-sleeved top**, a **green bracelet**, and a **light pink bow and heels**. Like Donald, Daisy doesn't actually wear bottoms, but instead shows off her white feathers. Again, the key is the color scheme: lilac, light pink, white, and yellow.

Model Abby Marrin (@parktimeprincess on Instagram) assembled her Daisy-inspired outfit (left) by pairing a lilac long-sleeved crop top from Forever 21 with a white denim miniskirt from H&M. She then accessorized with a light pink bow on top of her head.

Although Abby looks adorable by anyone's standards, if she were in a cosplay group with Mickey and his friends, her pink, white, and lilac outfit would instantly mark her as Daisy. Another great Daisy casual cosplay is modeled by actress Esther Lane (@itsestherlane on Instagram). She created a fashionable Daisy outfit (right) by wearing a light-pink-and-white-striped tank top underneath a fuzzy lilac cardigan with a yellow corduroy miniskirt. She then accessorized with a white belt, pink and gold bracelets, a pearl necklace, a pink headband, and a fuzzy pink crossbody bag.

This outfit is Daisy to a tee—not only does it follow her color scheme but it also displays her sassy fashionista energy.

Another way to style a Daisy Duck casual cosplay is with a white dress, a lilac cardigan, a pink bow, and pink shoes. I often see dress-and-cardigan Daisys on spring Dapper Day, as Daisy's colors match the season perfectly. For a more casual, everyday look, wear a comfortable lilac top with white shorts, yellow socks, a pair of sneakers, and a pink hair accessory. For a more masculine look, you can go with a men's collared shirt in lilac, white pants or shorts, and a pink belt and shoes.

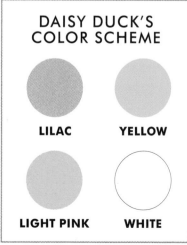

DAISY DUCK'S COLOR SCHEME

LILAC   YELLOW

LIGHT PINK   WHITE

GOOFY

The last of Mickey's close friends we'll channel is Goofy. The most popular way to cosplay this character is with a **bright orange long-sleeved turtleneck**, a **black vest**, **blue pants**, **brown shoes**, and a **green hat**. Goofy also has long floppy ears that some people like to incorporate into their look by putting their hair in ponytails. Goofy's outfit is the most casual of the bunch, easily replicated for any occasion. Instagrammer Hannah K. (@thatbabeintoyland) was able to create a nearly identical outfit (left) through a combination of items she already owned and some basics she found on Amazon. She wore an orange turtleneck crop top from Amazon, a black fringe vest from Tobi, and distressed mom jeans from Hollister, along with tan booties from JCPenney. She then accessorized with a pair of green transparent-frame glasses, also from Amazon.

If it's too warm to wear a turtleneck for your Goofy casual cosplay, though, any style shirt will do as long as it's bright orange and paired with blue bottoms and a green accessory. Model April C. (@trulyapril on Instagram) (right) chose an orange buttoned top tucked into a bright blue miniskirt for her Goofy casual cosplay. She then accessorized with a green scrunchie and double ponytails. An orange tank top worn with blue shorts, brown sandals, and a green bandanna would also be perfect for a summer Goofy.

Lastly, just like the rest of the outfits, Goofy's look can be dressed up. I often see men sport orange button-downs with green bow ties, black vests, blue pants, brown shoes, and green fedoras. I've also seen women wear orange tops with black cardigans, blue poodle skirts, brown heels, and green berets. When you stick to the color scheme for a character, the only limit is your imagination!

PLUS: floppy ears (or ponytails)

Goofy's Look

- Bright orange long-sleeved turtleneck
- Black vest
- Blue pants
- Brown shoes
- Green hat

CHAPTER 2
THE ROYAL TREATMENT
Princesses from Cinderella to Elsa

Aside from Mickey and Minnie, Disney princesses are the most common inspirations for casual cosplay. Since these characters are human, they're much easier to portray. As I mentioned earlier, at Disney theme parks, only children under the age of fourteen are allowed to wear actual Disney costumes—but as long as their outfits follow the general guidelines of casual cosplay, adults can easily dodge the rule. And, of course, there are plenty of places other than Disneyland where one might want to feel like a princess.

Snow White

Let's begin with Disney's original princess, Snow White. Her dress has a dark blue corsetlike top with light blue and red sleeves, a yellow skirt, and a white collar. She also sports yellow heels and a red headband with a bow. It sounds complicated, but casual cosplayers usually winnow it down to three primary colors and placements: blue top, yellow bottom, and red hair accessory. So, chances are, you already have what you need for this particular princess look! Fashion blogger Marina Ansaldo (@marinagracee on Instagram) (below) styled her Snow White look with items she already owned: a Cynthia Rowley velvet dress tucked into a yellow skirt from Forever 21. Underneath her dress, she wore a white collared shirt, also from Forever 21. To finish off the look, she accessorized with a red headband—again from Forever 21—and a pair of nude Lower East Side flats.

While Marina's outfit is a modern take on Snow White, vintage style blogger Curstie Marie (@missvintagelady on Instagram) put a retro spin on her casual cosplay (right). She often shops at vintage boutiques, and she found every piece for this ensemble either at those boutiques or on Etsy, a marketplace for vintage and handmade items. Curstie wore a navy blue top with white trim tucked into a yellow pencil skirt, then draped a red blazer over her shoulders to represent Snow White's red cape. She completed the look by wrapping a ribbon through her hair and fixing a bow at the top.

For a Disney-inspired look, this style is poised and professional. You could even wear it to work and see if any of your colleagues guess your secret princess identity!

Snow White's Look

- Blue top
- Yellow skirt
- Red hair accessory

Blue Peasant Dress Belle's Look

- Blue dress, jumpsuit, or overalls
- White long-sleeved T-Shirt
- PLUS: white apron

BELLE

Some princesses have multiple iconic outfits to choose from. For example, Belle from *Beauty and the Beast* has two very popular looks: her blue peasant dress and her yellow ball gown. Throughout most of the original movie, Belle wears a blue dress layered over a white long-sleeved blouse with a white apron around her waist and black flats. Her hair is tied back with a blue bow. Most casual cosplays of the character don't include the apron, but you can if it fits your style! One simple way to create a Belle casual cosplay is April C.'s pairing of a plain blue summer dress from Old Navy (left) over a solid white long-sleeved top from Target. She wears black flats and accessorizes with a blue bow in her hair, and she carries a yellow book to symbolize Belle's love of reading.

There are many ways to style the blue outfit—a dress, a top and jeans, even overalls—as long as you stick to the color scheme and placement. Belle's yellow ball gown, however, is all one color, so how can you communicate your specific princess preference? The details! Hairstyles, accessories, and props go a long way toward creating a great casual cosplay. Although at first it may feel odd to carry a prop around, if you're going to an event or taking photos, props and location can help a lot. April C. created a Belle casual cosplay (right) inspired by the yellow ball gown, but instead of a big, fanciful dress, she wore an off-the-shoulder maxi dress from SHEIN, put her hair up in a half bun reminiscent of how Belle wears hers in the film, and posed with a red rose. (In the original movie, a rose is pivotal to the plot, and has become synonymous with the character—so if you need a little something extra to boost your Belle outfit, add a rose detail!)

ARIEL

Another Disney princess with two distinctive looks is Ariel, star of *The Little Mermaid*. Ariel undergoes a major transformation in the film. In her mermaid form, she wears purple seashells on top and has a green tail on the bottom. After the sea witch grants Ariel's wish to become human, her signature outfit changes to a **big blue hair bow**, a **two-toned dress with a black or deep blue corsetlike top and a lighter blue skirt**, and a **white or light blue long-sleeved top**. (Due to variations in the color quality of the film, there are disagreements over the true colors of Ariel's dress.) However, as long as you style your outfit to include any combination of those colors in the proper places, your Ariel will be spot-on. Model Hali Simcoe (left) created her outfit by wearing a black tank top from Cotton On over a white long-sleeved shirt from Target, combined with a blue maxi skirt I found at a thrift store. (Unfortunately, the skirt had no tag, but blue maxi skirts are easy to find and cheap to purchase online.) To complete the outfit, she wore black flats and a blue bow in her hair.

For Ariel's mermaid form (top), I put together an outfit using a lilac crop top from Forever 21, a green circle skirt from H&M, and nude strappy sandals from Macy's. I then accessorized with a starfish hair clip to emphasize the mermaid vibe.

But if you're going for a more stylized look, you might want to go in the direction Abby Marrin took (bottom): she layered a green-and-white-striped summer dress over a purple sweater from Banana Republic, then accessorized with a red beret from Zara to evoke Ariel's red hair, a starfish hair clip, and a Danielle Nicole crossbody bag in the shape of a yellow-and-blue fish, reminiscent of Ariel's friend Flounder.

As you can see by contrasting these two looks, there are basic and high-fashion ways to portray the same character. It's all about what your style is, or what kind of clothes you have on hand. Also, though neither of us has Ariel's signature bright red hair, her color scheme is recognizable enough for most people to make the connection. Men can also style themselves in an Ariel-inspired outfit with a purple shirt and green shorts or pants (and nautical accessories for extra fun!).

Land Ariel's Look

- Big blue hair bow
- Two-toned dress with a black or deep blue corset and a lighter blue skirt
- White or light blue long-sleeved top

JASMINE

Like Belle, Princess Jasmine from the movie *Aladdin* is another character whose color scheme is hotly debated. Some Disney fans believe Jasmine's outfit—an off-the-shoulder crop top and matching harem pants—to be light blue, while others argue that it's closer to teal. Different illustrations or digital enhancements of the original film offer evidence for both—which is actually a good thing! It gives us more options when putting together looks inspired by the Arabian princess. Jasmine completes her monochrome ensemble with flats and a headband, all in the same mysterious shade, plus large gold earrings and a gold necklace. She's one of the only princesses who doesn't actually wear a dress, so she's a favorite of cosplayers who prefer two-piece looks.

PLUS:
gold accessories

PLUS:
hair tied in bubbles

The most popular Jasmine cosplay is a crop top and denim pants, but you can also switch the pants for joggers to achieve that loose-fitting look. You can even pair that same off-the-shoulder light blue or teal crop top with a matching skirt, as long as you include the gold accessories and signature hairstyle. Jasmine has very long, dark hair that she ties together in bubbles. You can create this effect by tying a low ponytail toward the back of your head, gathering a few inches of hair beneath the base of the ponytail, and tying another ponytail beneath that. Paired with a monochrome light blue or teal outfit and gold accessories, the look is unmistakably Jasmine's!

Disney fan Tara Lau (left) paired a teal jumpsuit with chunky gold earrings, a gold headband, and a tiger-striped clutch for her Jasmine casual cosplay. She also made sure to rock that bubble hairstyle!

Another great addition to a character-inspired outfit is a sidekick. Although Tara nails the Jasmine look on her own, when she gets together with Abby Marrin, who's dressed as Jasmine's tiger, Raja, it's a home run.

Abby's outfit is composed of a tiger-print sweater dress from Target, a gold pendant necklace, black loafers, and chic black sunglasses.

Duos and groups can take casual cosplay to the next level— and it's always more fun to do it with your friends!

I've also put together a much simpler, more casual Jasmine outfit for those who, like me, own mostly basics. My Jasmine-inspired look (above) is a blue bohemian maxi dress with gold accessories, nude gladiator sandals, and bubble hair.

Believe it or not, I do own a small magic lamp that I could carry around with me! But a more practical accessory to incorporate is a bag. I happened to already own an *Aladdin*-inspired bag with a little magic lamp detail, but you can also use a gold bag, a tiger-print one like Tara's, or one with a pattern resembling that of the magic carpet. Every detail counts! This is especially true when characters share very similar color schemes.

Jasmine's Look

- Monochrome light blue or teal outfit

CINDERELLA

Jasmine is not the only Disney princess clad in light blue. Cinderella is also most recognizable in monochromatic light blue, but her style is very different. Jasmine gives off a more bohemian vibe, while Cinderella's look is whimsical and soft. Cinderella is known for her light blue ball gown, the light blue headband that secures her updo, her black choker, and, of course, her glass slippers. I can't recommend wearing glass slippers, but if you have transparent heels, they'll work just as well. Most often, though, Cinderella cosplayers choose silver shoes to match the shine of her slippers in the film.

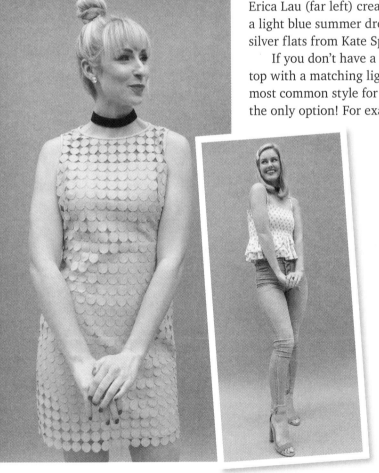

Since most occasions don't call for a ball gown, Disney enthusiast Erica Lau (far left) created her Cinderella casual cosplay using a light blue summer dress, a black choker, an updo, and sparkly silver flats from Kate Spade.

If you don't have a light blue dress, you can pair a light blue top with a matching light blue skirt. And while dresses are the most common style for Cinderella-inspired outfits, they're not the only option! For example, Abby Marrin put together a more casual look made up of a white-and-light-blue-polka-dotted tank top, blue jeans from Abercrombie & Fitch, a black choker, a white pearl barrette from H&M, and gray heels from Steve Madden.

Her outfit and accessories capture the spirit of Cinderella in a fun, laid-back way. Another casual option is a light blue sweater, light-wash jeans, a black choker, a silver handbag, and silver sneakers or flats.

Cinderella's Look

- Monochrome light blue outfit
- Clear, silver, or gray shoes

AURORA

There's one more Disney princess who wears a blue dress in her film, and that's Aurora from *Sleeping Beauty*. Aurora is a special case because there's no true color to her dress; the fairies that created it were never able to decide whether to keep it pink or blue. Therefore, an Aurora-inspired casual cosplay can be **pink, blue, or a combination of both**! An **off-the-shoulder long-sleeved dress or top** fits Aurora best, but it's not essential. If you don't have an off-the-shoulder top, you can wear a **white top** underneath your blue or pink one, since Aurora's dress has white trim on the top.

Aurora's Briar Rose outfit (which she wears while hiding from the evil fairy Maleficent) is also popular among casual cosplayers. The outfit consists of a white collared long-sleeved top, a black bodice, a gray skirt, and a black headband. As with many princess outfits, there are debates about the color of Briar Rose's skirt. Some depictions show it as gray, others as tan, some as blush, and some as lilac. Therefore, as long as you stay within that range of colors, you're bound to put together a fantastic look! Abby Marrin's Briar Rose look is made up of a white long-sleeved top layered beneath a black tank top, a blush maxi skirt, and a black headband. If you'd like to re-create this look, you can accessorize further with a purple shawl draped over your shoulders and a straw or basket-shaped bag.

Aurora's Look

- White long-sleeved top
- Black bodice
- Gray, tan, or blush skirt
- Black headband

ANNA

Now that we've covered the classic princesses, let's move on to the new generation. One cosplay crowd favorite is Anna from the movies *Frozen* and *Frozen II*. In the first film, Anna's silhouette is similar to that of Ariel in her blue ensemble, but Anna's color scheme is dominated by her two-toned dress, with its black bodice and dark blue skirt. Beneath the bodice she wears a light blue long-sleeved top, and she rounds out her outfit with a fuchsia cape and tall black boots. To re-create this look, Tara Lau (below, left) layered a black tank top over a light blue long-sleeved shirt, paired with a dark blue maxi skirt. She then draped a fuchsia cardigan around her shoulders to resemble Anna's cape, put her hair in pigtails, and donned black booties.

Another way to achieve this look is to wear the cardigan instead of draping it across your shoulders. If you wear the cardigan, you can just wear a plain black top underneath, with cobalt-blue bottoms and black footwear.

In *Frozen II*, Anna employs a slightly different color scheme. In this movie, she wears a black dress with a mustard-yellow turtleneck detail, a brown belt wrapped around her waist, tan pants or tights, a violet cape, and tall black boots. Vintage style blogger Curstie Marie (right) created her Anna-inspired casual cosplay by layering a black long-sleeved top underneath a yellow turtleneck and adding a purple shoulder cape overtop. For the bottom portion of the outfit, she wore a black miniskirt over black tights and black boots. To complete the look, she accessorized with a black beret and a gold belt around her waist. Another way to create an outfit based on Anna's *Frozen II* look is by wearing a black dress with a mustard-yellow turtleneck underneath, a brown belt around your waist, dijon-mustard-colored tights, an oversize violet cardigan, and black boots.

The other star of *Frozen* and *Frozen II* is, of course, Anna's older sister, Elsa. Elsa wears a number of different outfits in the films, but her signature color scheme is the icy combination of aqua blue, baby blue, and white. Erica L. (left) put together her Elsa-inspired casual cosplay by wearing a white sleeveless dress from New York & Company with a light blue blazer over it. She also added white and silver jewelry to recall Elsa's freezing powers and to add a bit of shine to the look. As a final touch, Erica styled her hair in Elsa's go-to side braid. This outfit is perfect if you're aiming for a mature look or dressing up for an event in a professional setting.

Frozen II Anna's Look

- Black dress
- Mustard-yellow turtleneck
- Brown belt
- Tan pants or tights
- Violet cape
- Tall black boots

MOANA

Our final princess, Moana, doesn't actually consider herself a princess, but she definitely embodies the spirit of a brave Disney heroine. Moana wears a **salmon-orange tube top with a dark orange tribal print** and a **light beige midi skirt over a straw petticoat** that peeks through the decorative openings in her overskirt. Lastly, Moana wears a **salmon-orange sash** around her waist to secure her skirt. Disney fan Kirsten Lopez (@curse_ten on Instagram) reimagined Moana's look (below) to fit her style by wearing a red tube top with beige loose-fitting pants, a white lace sash around her waist, and brown sandals. She then accessorized with a Kakamora crossbody bag from Danielle Nicole.

Despite not exactly matching Moana's look in the movie, Kirsten illustrated the character well by sticking to her color scheme and paying close attention to placement and detailing. However, there are ways to style a casual cosplay without the proper placement of colors and still portray the character well. Marina Ansaldo (right) switched up the color scheme by wearing orange shorts, a light beige top, and a light beige knit cardigan. She then accessorized with a woven choker necklace with a green pendant to represent the necklace seen in the film, a beige macramé crossbody bag, and brown sandals. And, of course, one of Moana's most distinctive aspects is her hair. Marina let down her long, dark, curly hair for this look, exactly as Moana does in the film.

At first glance, a Disney princess–inspired outfit may seem daunting, since most of them wear fanciful gowns or medieval attire. However, now that you know easy, modern ways to style each outfit, you can put together fun casual cosplays for any occasion. With so many Disney princesses to choose from—and surely more to come—you can dress as a princess every day!

Moana's Look

- Salmon-orange tube top with dark orange or red tribal print
- Beige midi skirt or orange shorts
- Straw petticoat
- Salmon-orange sash

PLUS: choker necklace with green pendant

PLUS: beige crossbody bag

PLUS: brown sandals

CHAPTER 3

BAD ACTORS & SECOND BANANAS

The Best of the Rest of Disney

Disney has a vast collection of other beloved characters that could easily inspire great casual cosplays, too. Although I couldn't possibly cover every character here, I do want to share some examples beyond the very popular princesses and Mickey and friends. For instance, Tinker Bell is a character still synonymous with Disney magic, even after all these years.

TINKER BELL (& PETER PAN)

Tinker Bell's color scheme is very simple: a **bright kelly-green strapless minidress** and **matching green slippers with white pom-poms**. Erica Lau (left) styled her Tinker Bell casual cosplay by wearing a kelly-green minidress and silver slippers with pom-poms. Although the dress isn't strapless, the shoulder ruffles serve as a reference to Tinker Bell's wings.

Erica completed her look by tying her hair up in a topknot, just as Tinker Bell does.

If you don't own a green dress, you can create your Tinker Bell cosplay by pairing a green tank top with a green miniskirt and your choice of either green or white shoes. Similarly, you can pair a green shirt, blouse, or any other kind of top with green shorts and green or white shoes.

Two other important details for this character's look are the hairstyle and the fact that Tinker Bell shows off her legs. If you were to pair pants or leggings with this look, it would be much more difficult—though not impossible—for people to understand your intent. My suggestion would be to stick to a green dress or skirt, or, if necessary, shorts.

Another reason I suggest wearing a dress or a skirt for Tinker Bell is because Peter Pan, the main character from the same movie, shares nearly the same color scheme, and without careful attention to detail, your Tinker Bell casual cosplay may be interpreted as Peter Pan instead. Peter also wears an all-green ensemble, but his is slightly different: instead of one solid color, Peter wears a lighter shade of green on top and a darker shade of green for his tights. He also sports a green hat with a red feather, a brown belt, and brown ankle boots. For her Peter Pan–inspired outfit, Abby Marrin (top) paired an emerald off-the-shoulder crop top with a pair of forest-green denim pants, and accessorized with a green beanie embroidered on the side with a red feather.

Compared to Erica's outfit, Abby's Peter Pan casual cosplay is clearly more masculine, distinguishing it from a Tinker Bell look.

This is not to say that all Peter Pan casual cosplays must lean masculine; after all, since at least 1904, he has often been played by a woman! Another example of an excellent Peter Pan casual cosplay is Kirsten Lopez's yellow button-down, which she altered to resemble the bottom half of Peter's shirt. She then wrapped a brown belt around her waist and wore a poodle skirt in a darker shade of green, and completed the look with a hat with a red feather.

Although this is more of a Dapper Day–inspired look, you can replace the poodle skirt with a dark green mini skirt and the heels with flats or sneakers to make it more mainstream.

Peter Pan's Look

- Light green or yellow top
- Dark green bottom
- Green hat with red feather
- Brown belt
- Brown ankle boots

CAPTAIN HOOK

For those looking to inspire an outfit after Peter Pan's arch nemesis, Captain Hook, the key elements are **red outerwear**, a **white top**, and **dark red or black bottoms**.

Disney fan Ali N. put together his casual cosplay by wearing a white collared button-down shirt with a black belt, red coat, and black pants. He also carried a foam sword. Another accessory you can add to your look if you did not want to hold a sword prop would be a floppy hat, possibly with a feather in it, like Hook's. Kirsten also arranged a Hook-inspired look by wearing a white button-down top with ruffle detailing, red long coat, black faux-leather pants, a black belt, black knee-high boots, and a black crossbody bag featuring the silhouettes of Peter Pan and Captain Hook. Although Captain Hook has a slightly more varied color scheme than Tinker Bell or Peter Pan, he does share these colors with other popular characters, including Mickey Mouse. The key to differentiating Captain Hook from other characters is the placement of the colors and attention to detail through accessories.

CAPTAIN HOOK'S COLOR SCHEME

WHITE RED BLACK

QUEEN OF HEARTS

The villainous Red Queen from *Alice in Wonderland* is another character with a black, white, and red color scheme.

In the classic 1951 animated film, she wears a black and red gown with a black and yellow chevron design peeking from beneath the skirt. However, the yellow chevron detailing is often left out of Red Queen–inspired looks, and replaced with copious amounts of heart detailing. There are many ways one can put together a Queen of Hearts casual cosplay, as long as hearts or cards are present. Karen and Long (@handsdowndisney on Instagram) put together a Queen of Hearts look that included a red short-sleeved top, black petticoat skirt, heart-patterned sheer black tights, and black heels. Karen and Long added accessories such as a red rose crossbody bag, heart-shaped wand, and a handmade headband. Other ways you can put together a Queen of Hearts inspired outfit is by wearing a solid red dress, black heels, and adding heart-shaped black or gold accessories. Again, despite the limited color scheme, the details are everything!

Queen of Hearts's Look

- Solid red or black top; or half red, half black top
- Solid red or black bottom; or yellow and black chevron bottom
- Red/Black accessories, especially heart and rose inspired

MALEFICENT

Yet another character with a limited color scheme is Maleficent, the seemingly evil godmother of Sleeping Beauty. In both the original animated and more recent live-action films, Maleficent wears an **all-black outfit**, but in the animated version, Maleficent's cloak has a **purple interior**, and **her skin is green**—both helpful details for a casual cosplay. In a subtle and comfortable nod to those facts, Erica Lau (below, left) wore a two-piece set from SHEIN with black, white, and green color blocks. She then added a pop of purple with an amethyst scrunchie in her hair and an orchid fanny pack worn across her torso. This look incorporates all of Maleficent's colors and serves as a covert casual cosplay while also being super on-trend!

But for those of you planning on heading to Disneyland in a Maleficent casual cosplay, I would suggest taking that extra step and wearing eye-catching Maleficent horns. These are sold at Disney parks, online, and in retail stores such as Hot Topic. You can also make your own horns, as I did, with some cardboard, black paint, tape, and a black headband. Model Hali Simcoe (below, right) created a casual cosplay inspired by the live-action version of Maleficent with a flowy black dress from Free People, a black choker necklace, and handmade horns.

ANIMATED MALEFICENT'S COLOR SCHEME

BLACK   WHITE

GREEN   PURPLE

SCAR

The last nonhuman Disney character we'll address is another villain: Scar from *The Lion King*. Scar is a bronze lion with a full black mane and green eyes. In the original animated film, Scar's fur sometimes comes off as rust-colored or burnt orange, so either bronze or orange is acceptable when putting Scar-inspired outfits together. Since most of his body is covered in fur, Hali wore a bronze jumpsuit accessorized with a furry black jacket draped around her shoulders to represent Scar's mane.

One final touch you can add to this look is a scar drawn over one of your eyes with either a pink or red makeup pencil.

An alternative Scar casual cosplay would be a rustic orange maxi dress paired with a black faux-fur coat or shawl, black boots, a black hat, and a dark makeup scheme. And if you're not interested in wearing a dress, a bronze long-sleeved shirt or sweater paired with black jeans, a faux-leather jacket, and combat boots would also be a suitable Scar casual cosplay, as long as you include the scar drawn over your eye with makeup. A men's Scar look could consist of a rust-orange baseball T-shirt with black sleeves, a pair of bronze shorts, a black beanie, and brown shoes.

Scar's Look

- Bronze long-sleeved shirt or sweater
- Black jeans
- Black leather jacket
- Black combat boots (or brown shoes)
- PLUS: black boots
- PLUS: black hat

PLUS:
black faux-fur
coat or shawl

CRUELLA DE VIL

A faux-fur coat or shawl would also come in handy for another Disney villain, Cruella de Vil. Cruella is the evil fashionista in Disney's *101 Dalmations* who's looking to make clothing out of dalmation fur. Although she's never actually seen wearing dalmation print in the movie, some Cruella cosplays incorporate the black-and-white print to represent her voraciousness. Her actual look in the movie is a plain black maxi dress with an oversize off-white fur coat, red heels, and red opera gloves. Staying true to this design, Tatum Blinn (below) styled her casual cosplay as a modern and classy take on the original outfit. She wore a black midi dress with a red belt wrapped around her waist, a white faux-fur jacket, and a pair of red heels, topped off with a red bag and red lipstick. This casual cosplay incorporates all of the details of Cruella de Vil's memorable look while still working as a fierce and fashionable outfit.

If you don't own a white faux-fur coat—and most of us don't!—you can always improvise. Tara Lau (right) used what she already had and paired a black-and-white-printed dress with a bright red coat and a tan faux-fur collar. She accessorized with a pair of black-and-white gloves, black-and-white hair ties, black sunglasses, and black heels. Although this look is very different from the one depicted in the movie, the color scheme is still correct, as is the style. Cruella de Vil would definitely wear this, so it works great!

Cruella de Vil's Look

- Black maxi dress
- White fur coat
- Red heels
- Red opera gloves

MARY POPPINS

This concept can also be applied to the beloved character Mary Poppins. In the original film, set in London in 1910, she wears multiple outfits that vary in color but stick to a very recognizable style for British nannies of the era: a white long-sleeved buttoned top paired with a navy skirt, a red bow tie, black tights, black booties, a long coat, a scarf, white gloves, and a black hat. One way I styled a Mary Poppins—inspired outfit was with a long-sleeved buttoned top with a ruffled lace design tucked into a black miniskirt over black tights and black booties (left). I then accessorized with a red ribbon as a bow tie and a black beret.

Fashion blogger Marina Ansaldo (right) took a different approach to her Mary Poppins casual cosplay. She wore a white button-down from Amazon tucked into a faux-leather skirt from Garage Clothing under a red coat, also from Amazon. She then accessorized with a gray scarf and pearl earrings from Forever 21, and a black hat from Windsor. To finish off the look, she added black boots from Universal Thread and a black umbrella.

The umbrella is an iconic piece of Mary Poppins's look, as the classic scene from the film shows her floating away under her magical umbrella.

Mary Poppins's Look

- White long-sleeved button-down top
- Navy skirt
- Red bow tie
- Black tights
- Black booties
- Red coat, white gloves, black hat

ERIC

An unlikely character with a similar color scheme to that of Mary Poppins is Prince Eric from *The Little Mermaid*. Eric also wears a white long-sleeved shirt and navy bottoms, and he, too, has a touch of red in his look. Although the character's outfit is fairly basic, the inclusion of the red belt or sash that he wears around his waist is what makes him distinguishable. Disney fan Jake B. styled his Prince Eric casual cosplay with a white long-sleeved button-down, blue jeans, a red belt, and black boots.

If you're interested in putting together a more feminine Prince Eric–inspired look, you can pair a white top with a blue denim skirt, a red belt, and black booties. Although Prince Eric is popular enough on his own for your casual cosplay to be recognized, your look would stand out even more if you were part of an Ariel and Eric duo!

Eric's Look

- White long-sleeved shirt
- Navy or gray jeans
- Red belt or sash
- Black boots

GASTON

Another male Disney character who looks great with his princess counterpart is Gaston. Despite Gaston's being the villain of the movie, and the fact that he and Belle never actually hit it off, Belle and Gaston duos seem to be popular among Disneygoers. In the animated film, Gaston wears a long red shirt with a yellow collar, a brown belt with a gold buckle, black tights, and brown boots. Men can re-create this look by layering a red T-shirt over a yellow collared shirt and wearing black pants, a brown belt, and brown boots.

Tara Lau styled a more feminine version of Gaston by pairing a statement red top with a black faux-leather skirt and black knee-high boots. She then added the yellow detail with a yellow belt and gold earrings. When dressed as Gaston, be sure to boost your confidence levels tenfold and show off those arms!

Gaston's Look

* Red shirt with yellow collar
* Brown belt with gold buckle
* Black tights
* Brown boots

ESMERALDA

Finally, for those interested in creating casual cosplays based on less-popular but still recognizable characters, I've gathered a few ideas for you to work with. First, let's look at Esmeralda, from the movie *The Hunchback of Notre Dame*. For those unfamiliar with the character, she's the woman who befriends Quasimodo, the titular hunchback. Esmeralda wears a white off-the-shoulder top, a turquoise blue belt, a purple maxi skirt, a violet hip scarf, black flats, a purple headband, and gold hoop earrings.

Even with these many elements, I found I already owned everything needed to replicate her look. I wore a white off-the-shoulder peasant top paired with a purple maxi skirt, both from thrift stores. I then accessorized with a purple fabric belt that I'd turned into a headband, a light blue hip scarf I'd also found at a thrift store, and gold hoop earrings. Another way you can create an outfit based on Esmeralda is by pairing a white top with a purple denim or circle skirt, a turquoise belt, a purple headband, and black or nude flats.

Esmeralda's Look

- White off-the-shoulder top
- Purple maxi skirt
- Turquoise belt or violet hip scarf
- Black flats
- Purple headband
- Gold hoop earrings
- Black or nude flats

LEWIS

This next character, the star of the Disney movie *Meet the Robinsons*, is still fairly unknown and underrated when it comes to casual cosplaying and Disneybounding. Lewis is a twelve-year-old boy with spiky blond hair and a brightly colored outfit: a **white collared shirt** under a **cobalt-blue sweater vest**, **red shorts**, **white tube socks**, **brown shoes**, and **round glasses**.

A Lewis-inspired look is easy to create, since all the elements that make up his outfit are available on Amazon for an affordable price. If you don't want to purchase any new items and want to use what you already own, you can pair a cobalt-blue collared shirt with red shorts, white tube socks, black sneakers, and round glasses and still produce an excellent Lewis casual cosplay!

A more feminine version of this look could incorporate a blue tank top layered over a white shirt, a red skirt, white tube socks, brown booties, and round glasses. Fashion blogger Curstie Marie added a vintage spin to her Lewis casual cosplay by wearing a white long-sleeved collared shirt under a blue button-up short-sleeved top, red slacks, brown oxford heels, a red headband, and glasses.

Lewis's Look

- White collared shirt
- Cobalt-blue sweater vest
- Red shorts
- White tube socks
- Brown shoes
- Round glasses

KIM POSSIBLE

The last lesser-known Disney character we'll look at is Kim Possible, a crime-fighting teenager who's the protagonist of the Disney Channel show of the same name. Although she wears multiple outfits throughout the series, Kim's signature color scheme is a **black long-sleeved turtleneck crop top**, **loose-fitting army-green cargo pants**, **black gloves**, a **brown belt**, and **black shoes**.

As with Lewis, you can re-create this look precisely using simple basics. Instagrammer Alexandra Rita (@enchantedalexandra) put together a stunning Kim Possible casual cosplay that fits perfectly with her vibrant red hair! For her outfit, Alexandra paired a plain black shirt with brown cargo pants, accessorized with a green tactical belt and black gloves, and then finished the look with black combat boots.

Although the color of the pants and the belt are switched from what Kim Possible normally wears, anyone who's familiar with the character would immediately recognize this fierce look.

Kim Possible's Look

- Black long-sleeved turtleneck crop top
- Loose-fitting army-green cargo pants
- Black gloves
- Brown belt
- Black shoes

CHAPTER 4

A FRIEND IN ME

Pixar Characters from Woody to Sulley

In 1995, the digital animation studio Pixar burst onto the scene with the hit *Toy Story*, and it's never looked back. Pixar characters have become a staple of casual cosplay, and none more so than the *Toy Story* friends.

WOODY

The two main characters of *Toy Story* are Sheriff Woody and Buzz Lightyear. Woody is a cowboy and Buzz is a space ranger. Woody's outfit consists of a **long-sleeved yellow button-down with a red windowpane print**, a **black-and-white cowhide vest**, **blue jeans**, a **brown belt with a gold buckle**, **brown cowboy boots**, a **brown cowboy hat**, and a **red bandanna** tied around his neck.

Tara Lau (left) re-created this look by wearing a thrifted yellow buttoned shirt with white checkered outlining, a pair of blue jeans from Madewell, a brown belt from Free People, cowboy boots, and a brown cowboy hat. This casual cosplay is nearly perfect; a red bandanna would have sealed the deal. Regardless, as long as you have a yellow top (preferably checkered or plaid), a blue bottom, brown shoes, and a brown cowboy hat, you can pull off a Woody-inspired look.

I also put together a feminine version of a Woody casual cosplay (right) by pairing a yellow-and-white-checkered crop top from Forever 21 with a faux-denim circle skirt, a brown cowboy hat, and tan booties.

Another cute twist would be a yellow top with a denim miniskirt, a brown belt, brown boots or booties, a brown hat, a red bandanna or scarf, and a cowhide-print handbag. Other variations might include denim shorts, a red ascot, or a cowhide-print denim jacket.

Woody's Look

- Long-sleeved yellow button-down with red windowpane print
- Black-and-white cowhide vest
- Blue jeans
- Brown belt with gold buckle
- Brown cowboy boots
- Brown cowboy hat
- Red bandanna

BUZZ LIGHTYEAR

Woody's space ranger friend, Buzz Lightyear, is a bit harder to re-create, but he does have a recognizable color scheme: he wears a space suit that is mostly white with some light green, purple, red, blue, and black detailing. You can put together a simple Buzz casual cosplay by pairing a white top with a light green miniskirt and accessorizing with a purple necklace or ascot. You can also wear a green top beneath a purple cardigan with white pants, shorts, or a skirt, and a black belt around your waist. Erica Lau (right) styled her Buzz Lightyear casual cosplay with a retro 1990s windbreaker in purple, green, and magenta color blocks paired with a white denim miniskirt and a purple baseball cap.

There are so many possibilities for coordinating a Buzz Lightyear–themed outfit, but I would advise you to avoid arranging the look in such a way that it resembles Dopey from *Snow White*. Dopey has a very similar color scheme, and sometimes outfits that are intended to resemble Buzz actually look more like Dopey. To prevent this, make sure not to wear a purple beanie, a loose-fitting green cardigan, or any tan pieces with your Buzz casual cosplay. If you're going for a Dopey-inspired look, however, then make sure to include those details!

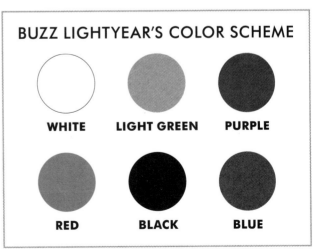

BUZZ LIGHTYEAR'S COLOR SCHEME

| WHITE | LIGHT GREEN | PURPLE |
| RED | BLACK | BLUE |

Bo Peep

There are also some great female characters in the Toy Story franchise. Bo Peep wears a couple of outfits throughout the series, the first being a **pink-and-white polka-dotted dress with a light blue bodice**, **blue pantaloons**, a **pink bonnet**, and **black flats**.

One way you can create an outfit based on this look would be to layer a pink cardigan over a light blue top and pair them with a white skirt with pink polka dots, then finish off the look with a pink beret or headband and black flats. Another option is a pink-and-white polka-dotted dress with a pink cardigan and black flats, accessorized with light blue details such as a belt or jewelry.

Bo Peep's second main outfit is a light blue jumpsuit with white lace detailing on the bodice, a pink belt around her waist, a large pink bow on the side of her head, and black flats. She also wears a purple cape that's occasionally incorporated into casual cosplays, but it's usually left out. Instagrammer Sasha C. (@prettymagical) (left) styled her Bo Peep casual cosplay by wearing a light blue jumpsuit from Forever 21 and accessorizing with a pink belt and a large pink bow.

Erica Lau (right) took a different approach to the jumpsuit in her Bo Peep–inspired outfit. She wore denim overalls with a light blue top underneath, and added a bright pink bow to the side of her head to finish off the look. Both Bo Peep outfits follow the same color scheme, so as long as you have a few basics in those colors, you can create any number of adorable Bo Peep casual cosplays!

Bo Peep #2's Look

- Light blue jumpsuit or denim overalls
- White detailing on bodice
- Pink belt
- Large pink bow
- Black flats
- PLUS: purple cape

JESSIE

Our final Toy Story character is Jessie, Woody's energetic cowgirl counterpart. Her outfit is a white button-down with a yellow color block on the chest and yellow cuffs, a pair of blue jeans with cowhide-print chaps, a brown belt with a gold buckle, brown cowboy boots, and a red cowboy hat.

Erica Lau (top) re-created this look with items she already owned—a white button-down shirt, blue jeans, and a black belt with a gold buckle. She then added a yellow bandanna around her neck and a red hat to perfectly channel Jessie.

Skyler Talley (@itssimplesky on Instagram) also put together a Jessie-inspired casual cosplay by wearing a white button-down shirt, red hat, and yellow bandana, but changed up the look by switching out the pants for a denim miniskirt and adding a cow-print purse inspired by the cowhide print on Jessie's pants. In the case of a gaudy or extravagant print, an accessory can really help in illustrating the character without your having to commit to larger articles of clothing you may not wear again. Also, once you have put your outfit together, if you would like to replicate Jessie's hairstyle, she sports a single braid with a yellow bow secured at the bottom.

Jessie's Look

- White button-down shirt
- Yellow bandanna
- Yellow cuffs
- Blue jeans
- Cowhide-print chaps
- Brown belt with gold buckle
- Brown cowboy boots
- Red cowboy hat

SULLEY

Monsters, Inc. is another Pixar classic with many characters to choose from. Although most of the monsters in the film don't actually wear clothing, they do have unique colors and patterns that can be replicated for fun casual cosplays. One of the main characters is Sulley, a teal, bearlike monster with light purple polka dots scattered over his furry body. He also has two small bone-colored horns on top of his head.

I put together a cozy Sulley casual cosplay by pairing a teal chunky-knit sweater with black leggings, purple socks, and white sneakers. You can also make this look a little more dressy by swapping out the sneakers for booties.

Another option for Sulley would be a light teal dress with a purple cardigan on top, a purple belt, and a light teal headband.

The ideal piece for a Sulley-inspired look would be a light blue or teal faux-fur jacket. Since those are pretty hard to come by, an easier route would be to pair a light blue or teal shirt with a slightly darker shade of leggings, purple socks or shoes, and a purple belt. For a more masculine Sulley casual cosplay, you can pair a teal or light blue collared shirt with a pair of teal or light blue shorts, then add a pop of purple with a belt or socks. Another way men can wear Sulley-inspired looks is with a light blue or teal button-down, purple shorts or pants, a light gray belt, and gray shoes.

PLUS:
teal headband

Sulley's Look

- Light blue or teal faux-fur top or dress
- Purple cardigan
- Dark leggings
- Purple socks
- White sneakers
- PLUS: purple or gray belt

MIKE WAZOWSKI

The other main character in *Monsters, Inc.* is Mike Wazowski. Mike is a strange-looking monster—just a ball with one giant eye, a mouth, two little horns, arms, and legs. His body is light green and his eye is blue. He doesn't usually wear any clothing, but sometimes appears in a blue Monsters, Inc. hard hat or a blue Monsters University baseball cap. Because Mike has a very limited color scheme, I would suggest incorporating the blue detail into his otherwise completely green look.

Hali Simcoe (left) created her Mike casual cosplay by wearing a lime-green summer dress with a blue cap so as to distinguish the look from, say, Tinker Bell.

If you don't have a lime-green dress, you can still put together a Mike Wazowski–inspired outfit by wearing a lime-green two-piece set. Erica Lau's set (right) is from SHEIN, and she also made sure to wear the blue MU baseball cap that she purchased at Disneyland.

Another option for a Mike casual cosplay is a lime-green top, a bright green skirt, green or gray booties or sneakers, and a blue beret or headband.

Mike Wazowski's Look

- Bright green outfit
- Blue cap, headband, or beret
- Green or gray booties or sneakers

Boo's Look

- Oversize pink shirt
- Lilac leggings
- White socks or shoes
- Double ponytails tied with pink hair ties

Boo

The last *Monsters, Inc.* character we'll look at is Boo, the small child that Mike and Sulley care for throughout the film. Boo wears an **oversize pink shirt, lilac leggings, white socks,** and **double ponytails tied with pink hair ties**.

I put together a Boo casual cosplay (left) by wearing a pink chunky-knit sweater with a pair of lilac leggings from Amazon. I then wore white Keds and put my hair into two ponytails. You could also wear an oversize pink shirt instead of the chunky sweater.

I put together a second Boo-inspired look (top, right) by pairing the same lilac leggings with a light pink dress from Forever 21. Since Boo's shirt is short-sleeved, I added a white short-sleeved top to add more coverage to the spaghetti-strap dress.

Another way you can put together a Boo casual cosplay would be a pink short-sleeved top with a lilac skirt, white high-top Converse sneakers, and double ponytails.

However, if you wanted to base your look off the monster costume Boo briefly wears in the movie, you would use a different color scheme. The monster costume is a purple material with a scaly texture, as well as beige-colored leather and ropelike material. Boo looks as though she is in a purple sleeping bag with beige tentacles for arms and legs, beige hair made out of rope, and googly eyes on top of her head. Although this may sound difficult to replicate, Sklyer Talley (bottom, right) creatively styled her outfit by layering a beige short-sleeved shirt underneath a purple sequin tube top tucked into a beige skirt. She then accessorized with a Mike Wazowski coin purse attached to her waist and a purple Wazowski Mickey-ear headband that also had googly eyes and rope detailing. Now, if you would like to re-create this look but are not necessarily heading to Disneyland or able to whip up your own pair of DIY Boo accessories, you can switch the Mickey ears for a purple or metallic-purple headband.

INSIDE OUT

Another Pixar movie with plenty of fun characters to choose from is *Inside Out*. In the film, emotions are personified by various eponymous characters: Joy, Sadness, and so on. Each emotion/character has a distinctive color, but because the film isn't as popular as other Pixar movies, these characters are most recognizable when in a group. So if you're interested in putting together a group casual cosplay, *Inside Out* characters are a great choice! Even two people dressing as the main duo, Joy and Sadness, will be recognized more easily than one person dressed as a single emotion.

JOY

Joy has blue hair and wears a sleeveless chartreuse summer dress. Since chartreuse is a yellowish-green color, sometimes casual cosplayers will go with yellow or lime-green dresses for Joy; either one works. For example, Tara Lau (right) put together her Joy-inspired outfit by wearing a yellow summer dress from Draper James, yellow heels, a blue beret, and a big smile!

Similarly, Instagrammer Kristina Guliasi (@magicallykristina) (below) sports a yellow apron dress with a yellow fabric belt tied in a bow at the front, accessorized with a yellow headband, yellow heels, and, again, a big smile.

Joy's Look

- Bright yellow dress
- Blue hair accessory
- A joyful smile

SADNESS

The character of Sadness wears a light blue–gray turtleneck sweater, blue pants, black flats, and round glasses with dark blue frames. Abby Marrin styled her Sadness casual cosplay by pairing a blue-gray knit sweater with blue jeans and gray heels. She then accessorized with a blue scrunchie around her wrist and a pair of black-framed glasses.

Although Sadness's sweater is a light blue–gray hue, a light blue, gray, or even white sweater will work when portraying the character. For example, Kristina Guliasi (right) put together her Sadness-inspired outfit with a chunky off-white sweater, dark blue skinny jeans, and black booties. She then accessorized with a blue beanie, round glasses, and blue lipstick.

Sadness's Look

- Light blue or gray turtleneck sweater
- Blue pants
- Black or gray shoes
- Round glasses with dark blue frames

DISGUST

Disgust is another key character in the film. She wears a dark green dress over tights in a darker shade of green, along with a purple ascot and purple flats. You can easily put together a Disgust casual cosplay with a jewel-neckline green dress, a purple ascot, and a whole lot of attitude. Erica Lau created her Disgust-inspired look with a plain white tank top underneath a green denim jacket, a matching green denim miniskirt, and a purple ribbon around her neck.

Another way you can put together a Disgust-themed outfit is by wearing a light green top with a dark green skirt or shorts, purple sneakers, and a purple scarf.

Disgust's Look

- Dark green dress
- Darker shade of green tights
- Purple ascot
- Purple flats

ANGER

Anger wears a white button-down shirt with a red tie and dark brown pants—but the character himself is red, so make sure to incorporate red into your Anger casual cosplay! You can create a look inspired by Anger either by wearing the same thing he does or by layering a red cardigan over a white top with black or dark brown pants and black flats. Another option would be to wear a white button-down with a brown miniskirt, a red ascot, black booties, and a red purse or other red accessory. I put together my Anger casual cosplay by wearing a red bodycon dress with white and black detailing, paired with red shoes and an angry face.

Anger's Look

- White button-down shirt
- Red cardigan
- Red tie
- Dark brown pants
- Black shoes
- PLUS: red purse or other accessory

FEAR

The last major emotion in the film is Fear. Throughout the movie, Fear, whose body is purple, wears a black-and-white houndstooth sweater vest over a light blue long-sleeved shirt with a red bow tie, black shoes, and dark purple pants. As with the other characters, you can easily re-create this look by purchasing every piece of Fear's outfit online, but there are also some great alternatives. You can channel Fear by wearing a black-and-white houndstooth or checkered dress over a light blue long-sleeved top with a red necklace and black shoes, accessorized with a purple purse, purple sunglasses, a purple hair clip, or purple jewelry. Hali Simcoe (top) put together her Fear casual cosplay using a black-and-white checkered jumpsuit, a purple blazer, and purple heels.

Fear's Look

- Black-and-white houndstooth sweater vest or checkered dress
- Light blue long-sleeved shirt
- Red bow or necklace
- Black shoes
- Dark purple pants

Again, these characters may not have very recognizable outfits compared to other Pixar characters, but they won't go unnoticed when grouped together!

KEVIN & RUSSELL

The last two Pixar characters I want to include are Kevin and Russell from the movie *Up!*

Kevin is a giant, ostrichlike multicolored bird that the main characters discover on their adventure. Kevin's feathers are an array of colors, most notably blue (on the neck) and yellow (on the chest). When putting a Kevin-inspired look together, be sure to incorporate a solid blue article of clothing toward the top of your outfit, as Maegan R did. Maegan (@missmbowtiquestyle on Instagram) (right) wears a solid blue jacket from Banana Republic, a rainbow dress from SHEIN, colorful heels from Popdaisies, a handmade bow from Missmbowtique, and a Kevin minibackpack from ShopDisney. You can also style a Kevin-inspired outfit by wearing a solid blue top and a multicolored rainbow skirt along with other colorful or feathered accessories. Kevin is a great character to choose if you love color!

Russell is a young boy with a Boy Scout look—he's clad in outdoor attire meant for hiking and exploring. He wears a yellow short-sleeved button-down with brown shorts, white tube socks, brown hiking boots, a yellow cap, an orange bandanna tied around his neck, and a brown sash around his torso that showcases his many badges. Instagrammer Hannah K. (left) created her Russell casual cosplay by pairing a yellow button-down from Amazon with tan paperbag shorts. She then accessorized with an orange bandanna around her neck and a Loungefly backpack inspired by the Wilderness Explorer pack Russell wears in the film.

Another way you can style a Russell casual cosplay is by wearing a yellow top with a brown skirt, an orange necklace, a yellow hat, and a brown crossbody bag to represent the sash he wears around his body.

Of course, there are many other characters from *Up* that you can base casual cosplays on, just as there are many more Pixar characters to choose from. For now, however, let's take a quick trip to a galaxy far, far away . . .

Russell's Look

- Yellow short-sleeved button-down
- Brown shorts
- White tube socks
- Brown hiking boots
- Yellow cap
- Orange bandanna
- Brown sash

CHAPTER 5

Far, Far Away

Star Wars Favorites

Whether you're a fan of the original trilogy, the newer films, or both, there are plenty of unique looks and iconic characters in the Star Wars family.

Leia

The original trilogy holds a special place in my heart, since my very first casual cosplay was Princess Leia. I re-created her famous all-white ensemble by pairing a white turtleneck top with a white maxi skirt, accessorizing with a silver belt and a pair of white sneakers, and styling my hair into two buns.

PLUS: hair in 2 buns

Although Princess Leia has several looks throughout the series, I chose to highlight this one because it's the most popular and one of the easiest to re-create. The color scheme is limited—just white and silver—but as long as it's styled appropriately (hairstyle included), all you have to do is wear an all-white outfit and a silver belt. I would suggest wearing long sleeves if you can find them—especially bell sleeves, because the all-white look with bell sleeves and space buns will instantly telegraph Princess Leia.

Leia's Look

- All-white ensemble
- Silver belt
- White sneakers

Han Solo

Princess Leia's beau, Han Solo, is also easy to cosplay. Han's signature outfit is an **off-white collared shirt**, a **black utility vest**, **dark blue pants with red detailing on the seams**, a **brown utility belt with a holster**, and **black boots**.

You could put together a great Han Solo outfit by gathering these exact articles, but if you want to be a bit more playful, you could wear a white shirt, a black denim vest, dark-wash jeans, a brown belt, and black boots. Erica Lau (above) created her casual cosplay by pairing a white long-sleeved top with a black vest, a black belt, a dark-wash denim skirt, and black knee-high boots.

Dark-wash pants or skirts both work for Han, as long as you don't skip the black vest. If you don't own one, you can use a sleeveless cardigan. As long as the white long-sleeved top is broken up by a black overlay, the force will be with you!

Han Solo's Look

- Off-white collared shirt
- Black utility or denim vest
- Dark blue pants or dark-wash jeans with red detailing
- Brown utility belt with a holster
- Black boots

Chewbacca

Han Solo's best friend, Chewbacca, is a tall humanoid creature with **varying shades of shaggy brown fur**. He doesn't wear anything other than a **brown bandolier** across his body, but you can still create fun Chewie casual cosplays.

One route is to wear a brown dress with a faux-fur vest, brown booties, and a brown crossbody bag. Hali Simcoe put together her Chewbacca casual cosplay by wearing a chestnut long-sleeved turtleneck top, khaki pants, brown boots, and a brown faux-fur jacket.

Star Wars–inspired props or accessories are also very helpful. In Chewbacca's case, he's synonymous with his ship, the *Millennium Falcon*, so Hali accessorized with a Disneyland popcorn bucket in the shape of the *Falcon* and a magnetic porg plushie secured on her shoulder. If a faux-fur vest or jacket will be too warm for you on the day of your casual cosplay, you can substitute with a dark brown fringe dress or a brown top and bottom with a fringed vest or jacket.

Chewbacca's Look

- Brown dress
- Faux-fur vest
- Brown booties
- Brown crossbody bag

Darth Vader

Another Star Wars character with a limited color scheme is Darth Vader. It's difficult to put together a casual cosplay for Vader because he basically wears all black: a **black jumpsuit** with a **black cape**, a **black belt**, **black armor**, **black gloves**, **black boots**, and a **black helmet that covers his entire head and face**. The one splash of color are the buttons on the box he wears on his chest to control various aspects of his suit; you can incorporate these colors into your casual cosplay by wearing silver or red jewelry.

Hannah K. styled her Darth Vader casual cosplay by wearing a black jumpsuit she purchased from Amazon and a silver belt around her waist.

The clues that tell you this is a Vader look are her open, flowy sleeves, which recall a cape. You'll need to incorporate details like capes, gloves, or handbags to clearly communicate that your outfit is meant to be inspired by Darth Vader.

Darth Vader's Look

- Black jumpsuit
- Black cape
- Black or silver belt
- Black armor
- Black gloves
- Black boots
- Black helmet
- PLUS: silver or red jewelry

PLUS:
gold belt, jewelry,
sunglasses

PLUS:
metallic jacket

C-3PO

Star Wars droids are also popular characters for casual cosplay. C-3PO is all gold but has an exposed midsection that shows his colorful internal wiring. One way to create a C-3PO-inspired look is to wear a gold tank top, a gold skater skirt, a black belt, gold flats, and gold jewelry, and carry a gold handbag. You can also substitute a gold dress for the top and skirt.

For those uninterested in wearing a skirt or a dress, you can construct a stunning C-3PO casual cosplay the way Erica Lau did, by pairing a mustard-yellow buttoned top with khaki pants, a metallic jacket, a gold belt, gold jewelry, and sunglasses with gold frames.

Here's another perfect example of a casual cosplay that's formal enough to wear to the office yet is still perfectly representative of the character.

C-3PO's Look

- Gold tank top or dress
- Gold skirt or khaki pants
- Black belt
- Gold flats
- Gold handbag

R2-D2

The other popular Star Wars droid that often goes together with C-3PO is R2-D2. R2's color scheme is **white, blue, and silver**. Most of his body is white metal, with blue and silver detailing. You can style an R2-D2-inspired outfit by wearing a white-and-blue striped top with a pair of white or blue shorts or a skirt. You can then finish off the look with gray sneakers or silver flats. Abby Marrin put together her R2-D2 casual cosplay by wearing a white-and-blue porcelain-print set from SHEIN.

The blue design over the white base of the set resembles the blue detailing on R2. Abby then accessorized with silver jewelry and a silver crossbody bag. Men can create an R2-D2 casual cosplay by pairing a plain white shirt or button-down with a blue bow tie, white shorts or pants, a blue belt, blue shoes, and a blue hat. To further accentuate the idea that you're dressed as R2-D2, pair up with a fellow casual cosplayer who's channeling C-3PO!

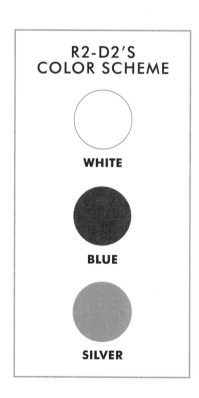

R2-D2'S COLOR SCHEME

WHITE

BLUE

SILVER

BB-8

And if you'd like to make that duo a trio, the recent Star Wars trilogy introduces a new droid, BB-8. BB-8's color scheme is similar to that of R2-D2, but with orange instead of blue. You can put together a casual BB-8 cosplay by wearing a white top with an orange skirt or shorts, silver shoes, and orange accessories. You can also wear a white dress with an orange belt, an orange beret or other hair accessories, an orange cardigan, and gray or silver shoes.

Erica Lau created her BB-8 casual cosplay by wearing an orange-and-white Kate Spade dress with silver flats and statement earrings.

If you and two friends are interested in a trio cosplay, these three droids would be a clever choice!

BB-8'S COLOR SCHEME

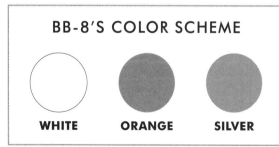

WHITE   ORANGE   SILVER

Not only do the earrings follow BB-8's general color scheme but they're also round, just like the little droid itself.

Kylo Ren

Another new character from the recent Star Wars installments is Kylo Ren, the grandson of Darth Vader. Like his grandfather, he wears an **all-black ensemble**, which makes it a challenge to effectively channel him. His outfit consists of a **black tunic** with **black leather pants**, a **black belt**, **black boots**, **black gloves**, a **cloak**, a **hooded scarf**, and a **helmet that covers his head and face**. As with Vader-inspired cosplays, you can wear all black with red accessories that represent their red lightsabers. There are a couple of details, however, that can differentiate your Kylo Ren–inspired casual cosplay from a Darth Vader one, such as a hooded scarf and a red scar drawn across your face.

Tara Lau created her Kylo Ren outfit by wearing a black jumpsuit from Express, a black waist belt, a long black cardigan, black knee-high boots, black opera gloves, and black jewelry. She then completed the look with a lightsaber, making it crystal clear that she was dressed as a Star Wars character! (If you're not on your way to Disneyland or Comic Con, though, the outfit still works without the lightsaber.)

Kylo Ren's Look

- Black tunic
- Black leather pants
- Black belt
- Black boots
- Black gloves
- Cloak
- Hooded scarf
- Helmet
- PLUS: red accessories

Rey

Lastly, the beloved protagonist of the new Star Wars trilogy is Rey. Rey's color scheme varies slightly throughout the films but stays within a small range of neutral shades—tan and brown, gray and brown, or white and brown. All her outfits consist of a shirt or tunic worn under long fabric that's draped over and across her body, with capri pants, boots, and wrapped sleeves. Although the wrapped sleeves are a Rey signature, they may be difficult to create from what you have in your closet, so it's understandable if you leave them out. If you don't want to wrap a scarf or fabric across your body, you can still put together a Rey-inspired look without that!

Rey's most popular color scheme is tan and brown, so the outfit ideas that follow use those colors, but you can always switch it up with white or gray. One way to create a Rey casual cosplay is to wear a white tank top with tan paperbag pants, brown boots, and a long tan cardigan. For this look, you want the cardigan to be flowy, and to reach at least to mid-thigh. And don't forget Rey's hairstyle, a very important detail that's become synonymous with her character: three buns stacked vertically up the back of her head. Hali Simcoe (left) styled a Rey-inspired outfit by wearing a flowy tan dress from Free People, brown booties, and Rey's signature three-bun hairstyle. She also carried a lightsaber.

Although Rey never actually wears a dress, the color and style of the dress Hali wears echoes Rey's look perfectly, and is a rare twist on a Star Wars character that feels very modern. Because most Star Wars characters tend to wear loose, neutral-colored clothing, casual cosplay can be a challenge, but you can do a lot with hairstyles and accessories to really make your outfits stand out!

Rey's Look

- White shirt or tunic
- Capri pants
- Brown boots
- Wrapped sleeves
- PLUS: long tan cardigan

CHAPTER 6

WORLD OF WIZARDRY

Everything Harry Potter

In the world of Harry Potter, young wizards attend a prestigious school of wizardry called Hogwarts. On the first day of school, each new student is sorted into one of four houses—Gryffindor, Slytherin, Ravenclaw, or Hufflepuff—based on their personalities, goals, passions, and ambitions. Each house has its own set of values and characteristics, as well as its own color scheme: Gryffindor's colors are **scarlet and gold**, Slytherin's are **green and silver**, Ravenclaw's are **blue and bronze** (except in the films, where they're **blue and gray**), and Hufflepuff's are **yellow and black**. Unlike outfits inspired by specific characters, casual cosplay inspired by a Hogwarts house allows for so much more flexibility! As long as you stick to the colors of each house and mix them only with neutral colors such as black or white, you can't go wrong.

GRYFFINDOR

The students of Gryffindor are deemed daring and courageous, which is why their color scheme is bright and bold: red, black, yellow, and white. One way I've put together a Gryffindor-inspired look is by pairing a white tank top with a dark red pleated skirt from H&M, a long black cardigan from Brandy Melville, yellow socks from Amazon, black slip-on sneakers from Steve Madden, and a scarlet handbag from BoxLunch.

Another way to create a Gryffindor casual cosplay is with a red long-sleeved top, black denim pants, red Converse sneakers, and a gold hair accessory or jewelry. Men can take a page from Jake B. (right), who layered a black long-sleeved shirt over a white collared shirt with light-wash gray jeans, black boots, and a red-and-black gradient scarf. (House scarves are a staple of Hogwarts-inspired looks.) The last detail Jake added to his Gryffindor casual cosplay was a wand—something no budding wizard would ever be caught without!

Gryffindor's Look

- White top
- Scarlet bottom
- Black cardigan or cape
- Yellow accessories

SLYTHERIN

Slytherin is occupied by students with clever wit and ambition who are often seen as intimidating, tough, and sometimes even evil—and though this isn't really borne out by the text, Slytherin-inspired looks tend to lean toward grunge or goth styles as a result. One example would be a black crop top, black ripped jeans, fishnet tights, black combat boots, a black beanie, and a dark green bomber jacket. However, as with any outfit, I encourage you to put your own personality into it.

For my Slytherin-inspired outfit, I paired a black bell-sleeved top with a dark green plaid skirt, gray socks, black booties, and a black hat to create a girly, preppy look that fits with my everyday style. On the other hand, Instagrammer Alexandra Rita (right) wanted to show off that strong Slytherin personality, and styled her look with a green plaid blazer and pant set from MakeMeChic, a green long-sleeved top from Forever 21, black heels from Aldo, a green crocodile-skin handbag from ROMWE, and a Hogwarts wand from the Wizarding World of Harry Potter at Universal Studios. This fierce outfit gives off the perfect boss-witch vibes that every true Slytherin aims for.

Slytherin's Look

- Black crop top
- Green plaid blazer
- Black ripped jeans or dark green plaid skirt
- Fishnet tights
- Black combat boots or heels
- Black beanie
- Dark green bomber jacket
- PLUS: green handbag

RAVENCLAW

Students sorted into Ravenclaw value wisdom and creativity. For the most part, Ravenclaw outfits lean preppier; one way to style a Ravenclaw outfit is by wearing a navy-blue long-sleeved top with a blue-and-gray-plaid pleated skirt and a navy or gray headband. You can also wear a gray dress with a navy cardigan, a navy belt, and a gray beret.

Abby Marrin created her Ravenclaw casual cosplay by pairing a long-sleeved gray turtleneck top with a blue denim skirt, black tights, black boots, a long black cardigan, and a Ravenclaw scarf from Hot Topic.

The scarf follows the film version of the Ravenclaw color scheme; if you want to base your casual cosplay on the original Ravenclaw colors from the book, however, you would need to switch out the gray for bronze. Although most retailers sell blue-and-gray Ravenclaw merchandise, you can find handmade and custom items such as scarves, pins, and other accessories that follow the book's color scheme on Etsy and similar sites. A Ravenclaw look based on these colors might be a navy-blue sweater with a brown or bronze skirt, a brown crossbody bag, and brown boots. You can also wear a blue top under a brown cardigan with a black skirt, a brown belt, and brown booties. Both color combinations are acceptable and appealing, so pick the one you like most!

Ravenclaw's Look

- Gray top
- Blue bottom
- Black cardigan or cape
- Blue-and-gray scarf

HUFFLEPUFF

Last but not least is Hufflepuff, whose students value loyalty, kindness, and honesty; in my humble opinion, Hufflepuff might be the most underrated Hogwarts house. Hufflepuffs are often portrayed as kind and docile, but they can definitely be tough and even intimidating when they need to be. As I mentioned earlier, this house's colors are yellow and black, so one version of a Hufflepuff casual cosplay could consist of a black tank top, a black cardigan, a yellow pleated skirt, yellow socks, and black slip-on sneakers. You could also just wear a yellow summer dress and accessorize with black jewelry, a black headband, and black shoes.

April C. (right) created her Hufflepuff casual cosplay using a yellow bell-sleeved top from Forever 21, a black-and-white pleated skirt from Brandy Melville, sheer black tights, black boots, and gold jewelry.

Another great thing about casual cosplays based on Hogwarts houses is that placement doesn't matter as much as it does with an actual character. For example, you can wear the same outfit April wore but switch the colors so that you're wearing a black top with a yellow skirt. A third option is a black tank top with a pair of black skinny jeans, yellow Converse sneakers, a yellow jacket, and a yellow beret, headband, or beanie.

Hufflepuff's Look

- Black tank top or yellow dress
- Black cardigan or yellow jacket
- Black-and-white pleated skirt
- Yellow socks
- Black shoes
- PLUS: black, gold, or yellow jewelry, black or yellow headband, yellow beret or beanie

PLUS:
black tights

HARRY POTTER

Hogwarts students may have to wear uniforms while at school, but that doesn't mean there aren't characters who have distinct looks! Harry Potter is usually wearing either his Hogwarts uniform or a plain shirt, a zip-up jacket, jeans, and sneakers—all of which aren't very notable by themselves. But once you add the pertinent details to a Harry Potter casual cosplay, you'll be recognizable as his character specifically instead of just another Gryffindor student.

Harry Potter's Uniform Look

- White button-down
- Black skirt
- Scarlet scarf or tie
- Black round glasses
- Black shoes
- PLUS: buttoned-up gray cardigan
- PLUS: curly hair, scar

Harry's specific features include his unruly curly hair, round glasses, and the scar on his forehead. Hali Simcoe (left) put together her Harry Potter casual cosplay by incorporating those details (minus the scar): she wore a white button-down tucked into a black skirt with a scarlet scarf to resemble Harry's school uniform, then made sure to curl her hair and accessorize with round glasses.

None of what Hali is wearing is official Harry Potter merchandise, but if you'd like to go that route, pop-culture retail stores like Hot Topic, BoxLunch, and even Target carry Hogwarts scarves, ties, cardigans, and more. For men, re-creating a Harry Potter look is as easy as pairing gray pants with a white button-down, a scarlet tie, round glasses, black shoes, and a buttoned-up gray cardigan—though there's plenty of official Harry Potter attire available for men as well.

LUNA LOVEGOOD

If you want to base your casual cosplay on an outfit one of the characters wears when not in uniform, merchandise won't help as much. Luna Lovegood is a Ravenclaw, and throughout the films she's seen wearing her normal school uniform: a collared white button-down under a dark gray cardigan with a blue-and-silver tie, a black skirt, black tights, and black shoes—but this isn't the outfit she's most known for. The most recognizable Luna ensemble is a pink tweed blazer, a black dress with a colorful splatter design, bright blue leggings, blue striped socks, pink sneakers, and wacky pink glasses.

PLUS: book or magazine

As wild as that combination sounds, Abby Marrin put together a similar outfit with things she already had in her closet. She wore a pink tweed blazer, dark blue polka-dotted shorts, black tights, plain blue socks, pink high-top Converse sneakers, and pink tinted glasses.

Although Luna's outfit has a lot going on, there is still a clear color scheme. When styling your own Luna casual cosplay, be sure to wear some sort of pink outerwear, a dark blue or black top, a dark blue or black skirt with a pattern on it, blue or black tights, blue socks, pink shoes, and pink glasses. In terms of props, she's a big reader, so if you carry around a book or a magazine along with your wand, you won't be mistaken for anyone else.

Luna Lovegood's Look

- Collared white button-down
- Dark gray cardigan
- Blue-and-silver tie
- Black skirt or shorts
- Black tights
- Black or pink shoes

- Pink tweed blazer
- Black dress with colorful splatter design
- Bright blue leggings (or blue or black tights)
- Blue striped socks
- Pink sneakers
- Wacky pink glasses

DOLORES UMBRIDGE

The last Wizarding World character we'll look at is among the most hated in the Harry Potter universe: Dolores Umbridge. Although she's a villain, Potter fans love to hate her (and still appreciate her style). She always sports an **all-pink look**, either monochromatic or a mix of different shades. Her vibe is **vintage**, with lots of dresses, cardigans, and long coats; she basically dresses like a snooty, wealthy older woman from the 1930s.

Alexandra Rita (left) put together her Umbridge casual cosplay with a fringe-trim tweed jacket and skirt set from SHEIN, a white blouse, pink flats, and pearl accessories.

Tweed jackets and skirts are easy to find at thrift stores, since tweed was a popular material decades ago. Luckily it's coming back into style, so you can also shop online for an Umbridge-inspired pink look. If you're not a fan of tweed, you can wear a light pink jewel-neckline dress under a cardigan in a darker shade of pink, heels in that same shade, and pink accessories, finished off with a 1930s updo and a wand.

Whether you love a character, love a house, or love to hate a nemesis, these magical looks will transport you straight into the wizarding world of Harry Potter!

Dolores Umbridge's Look

- Light pink jewel-neckline dress or skirt set
- Darker pink cardigan
- Long coat
- Pink flats
- Pearl accessories

CHAPTER 7

LEAGUE OF HEROES

Marvel & DC Comics

Superheroes and their foils have been popular since they debuted in comic books, and have become even more popular through various television shows and full-length films. Although there is a plethora of comic book companies, the two biggest fish by far are Marvel Comics and DC Comics. Marvel, in particular, has reached stratospheric heights since it started producing blockbuster adaptations of its comics in 2008. The first Marvel Studios film, *Iron Man*, was so successful that they have released twenty-two more since then, giving even the less-popular characters within the universe time to shine.

DC Comics has also made plenty of TV shows and movies starring its own superheroes, especially their most popular trio: Superman, Batman, and Wonder Woman. All have undergone various makeovers through the years, which is nice because they allow for greater flexibility in putting together creative cosplays.

IRON MAN

Let's start with the man who lit the fuse of the Marvel resurgence: Iron Man. Iron Man's true identity is billionaire Tony Stark, an arrogant genius who loves to wear expensive suits and large sunglasses. For men, the best way to re-create a Tony Stark look would be to wear a suit and tie, a pair of Flight .006–style aviator sunglasses, and a goatee.

IRON MAN'S COLOR SCHEME

SCARLET **GOLD** **BLACK**

The Iron Man suit is made of red metal with gold detailing, so for a casual cosplay of the machine character, you could pair a yellow shirt with red shorts or pants, a black belt, black shoes, a red faux-leather jacket, and a gold watch. Also, if you wanted to combine the two looks, you could wear a red suit with a gold tie, a gold belt, and the signature sunglasses. Women can create an Iron Man casual cosplay by wearing a black tank top underneath a red faux-leather jacket with gold leggings or pants, red booties, gold jewelry, and a pair of flashy sunglasses. April C. (left) put together her Iron Man casual cosplay using a red off-the-shoulder top from Forever 21, a gold circle skirt from Amazon, a scarlet velvet blazer from ASOS, black booties, gold jewelry, and a pair of Ray-Ban sunglasses.

The color combination and the velvet blazer reference Stark's fancy style, though the outfit itself cost less than fifty dollars. Another way you can style an Iron Man casual cosplay is by wearing a red dress and accessorizing with gold statement earrings, a gold necklace, gold bracelets, a gold handbag, and gold heels. When putting together an Iron Man–inspired outfit, try to avoid substituting flat yellow and red for gold and scarlet, or the intent will be lost. It's the metallic accents and textures that call to mind the shine of Iron Man's suit.

BLACK WIDOW

Another key member of the Avengers squad is Natasha Romanoff, otherwise known as Black Widow. This highly skilled agent typically wears a **black leather bodysuit with a tactical belt**, **holsters**, **attached weapons**, and **black leather boots**.

However, if you don't want to squeeze into an undoubtedly uncomfortable (and warm) bodysuit, you can opt for a much more wearable option. Skyler Talley styled her Black Widow casual cosplay by wearing a black long-sleeved top with a red Black Widow graphic symbol printed on the chest, along with a pair of black faux-leather shorts and black combat boots. She then finished the look by accessorizing with a Black Widow backpack from Loungefly. Although it may be difficult to make an all-black outfit resemble Black Widow, the key elements that made Sky's outfit fantastic for this character are her inclusion of faux leather and Black Widow's signature red symbol. However, if you do not have any clothing with a Black Widow symbol, you can also put together an outfit inspired by this Marvel hero by wearing black faux-leather pants or leggings, black combat boots, a red top, and black faux-leather jacket.

Black Widow's Look

- Black long sleeve top
- Black leather or faux-leather bottoms
- Black leather or faux-leather boots
- Red accessories

SPIDER-MAN

One of the most popular Marvel characters, Spider-Man was well-known even before the recent Marvel craze. Spidey wears a skin-tight red-and-blue bodysuit and face mask. His alter ego is teenager Peter Parker, an average-looking, nerdy high schooler. Although you can purchase a Spider-Man bodysuit online for less than eighty dollars, wearing it would be considered more full cosplay than casual cosplay. So, instead, we're going to combine a superhero suit with an average Peter Parker vibe.

Since Spider-Man's suit is mostly red and blue with some black web detailing, I created my Spider-Man look using a red knit sweater from Target, ripped blue jeans from Aéropostale, and red high-top Converse sneakers. I then added a Danielle Nicole Spider-Man crossbody bag.

Another option for accessorizing this outfit would be any spider-related jewelry, like a necklace with a spider pendant, a spider ring, spider earrings, etc. You can also style a Spider-Man casual cosplay by wearing a red tank top, a blue skirt, and red shoes, or by wearing a red dress, a blue cardigan, and red heels. Men can put together a Spider-Man look with a red shirt, blue shorts, and a pair of red high-top sneakers. For a dressier look—possibly for Dapper Day or a similar event—men can also wear a white button-down, a blue tie, a red blazer, and blue pants. To accentuate the idea that you're dressed as Spider-Man, you can even draw weblike stripes all over the blazer and wear a spider lapel pin.

Spider-Man's Look

- Red sweater or shirt
- Blue jeans, skirt, or shorts
- Red sneakers or heels
- Spider-related jewelry or bag

AGENT PEGGY CARTER

Unlike Iron Man and Spider-Man, Peggy Carter is a character who continues to fly under the radar even after appearing in a number of the recent Marvel films. This may be because she's never really shown in action; it's acknowledged that she's a skilled secret agent, but many fans know her primarily as Captain America's love interest. In the comics, however, it's clear that Agent Carter is a strong, intelligent woman who's more than capable of holding her own in combat.

She's often depicted wearing a collared white button-down under a navy-blue blazer and skirt set and her signature red fedora. You can re-create this look using your own navy suit, but a navy-blue pencil dress is a fun (and more versatile) alternative. Additionally, you can skip the blazer and just wear a white buttoned top with a navy skirt. As long as you incorporate the red hat, you'll have an Agent Carter look.

Another popular Agent Carter outfit is a white button-down under an army-green blazer and skirt set with gold detailing. If you don't have an army-green blazer, you can skip it and simply wear the white button-down with an army-green pencil skirt, a brown belt, and brown shoes. Curstie Marie (left) created her Peggy Carter casual cosplay using a dark brown denim jacket in place of the blazer, green high-waisted slacks, and brown heels. Curstie also incorporated Agent Carter's vintage curled hairstyle. Since this outfit doesn't include a signature accessory such as the red hat, distinctive hair does the job.

Agent Peggy Carter's #2 Look

- White button-down
- Army-green blazer and skirt set
- Gold detailing
- Brown belt
- Brown shoes or heels

CAPTAIN AMERICA

If you were looking to style an outfit inspired by Peggy Carter's love interest, Captain America, there are countless ways you can style his classic color scheme of red, white, and blue. His superhero outfit consists of a bodysuit that is mostly blue with a white star on the chest and a red-and-white-striped belly.

He also wears either brown or red boots and gloves and carries his signature red, white, and blue shield. One way to put together a Captain America outfit is to wear a red-and-white-striped top, blue jeans, a brown belt, and brown boots, and accessorize with a Captain America shield backpack. Skyler Talley styled her Captain America by wearing a red long-sleeved top, blue circle skirt, and white sneakers. She also added a crossbody bag designed after Captain America's shield, a handmade headband that also features Captain America's shield, and a necklace with the Avengers symbol as the pendant.

Captain America's Look

- Red top
- Blue bottom
- Red, white, and blue accessories

LOKI

Marvel heroes aren't the only fun casual cosplay subjects in the universe—there are plenty of wickedly good villains as well. Loki is among Marvel's most popular villains, though his outrageous outfits are nearly impossible to replicate: in the comics, he sports a bright green bodysuit, gold-and-black armor, a green cape, gold boots, and a gold helmet with long curled horns; in the films, he wears a black leather tunic with gold and dark green accents, black leather pants, black leather boots, a long black coat with dark green and gold accents, and a gold helmet with curled horns. So while it may be too much to match him piece for piece, there is a clear color scheme for a Loki casual cosplay: green, black, and gold.

One way men could put together a Loki-inspired look is by wearing a dark green shirt, black pants, a faux-leather jacket, a gold watch, and black boots. A more feminine Loki cosplay might be a black dress, a gold belt, sheer black tights, black knee-high boots, a long green cardigan, and gold jewelry. Tara Lau (left) created a classy Loki look with a dark green pencil dress, a gold belt, black pointed-toe heels, a black blazer slung over her shoulders, and gold jewelry. This outfit follows the color scheme perfectly and appears to be a normal, if sophisticated, ensemble, but is secretly nerdy.

One last example of a Loki-inspired look would be a black shirt with black faux-leather pants or leggings, black boots, gold jewelry, a gold headband, and a long green coat.

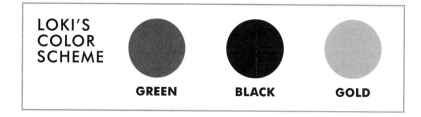

LOKI'S COLOR SCHEME

GREEN   BLACK   GOLD

THE JOKER

Naturally, DC Comics has legendary villains as well. The Joker is the arch-nemesis of DC superhero Batman; he is a lunatic, genius criminal mastermind with green hair and full clown makeup. The design of the character varies depending on the format, but the most recognizable Joker outfit comes from *Batman: The Animated Series*, where he sports a purple pantsuit, a yellow vest, a green bow tie, and purple gloves. Instead of dying your hair green and donning white face paint, you can put together a Joker casual cosplay by wearing a yellow button-down under a purple blazer with purple or black slacks, black shoes, green jewelry, and green accessories. You can also wear a green dress, purple tights, black heels, yellow jewelry, and a purple coat.

PLUS: red lipstick

Men can wear a toned-down version of the Joker's outfit that's more suitable for everyday wear by pairing a purple button-down with a green necktie or scarf, black pants, black gloves, and black shoes. For her Joker casual cosplay, Tara Lau (left) layered a yellow denim jacket buttoned up to the collar over a white buttoned top, then added a purple blazer and paired it with a green denim skirt. Finally, she accessorized with a yellow belt, white statement earrings, and red lipstick to resemble Joker's bright red lips. Although this outfit is a wild combination of colors, it still works, since it gives a nod to the Joker's color scheme while still being ready for a night on the town.

One last option for a Joker-inspired look is a green button-down with a buttoned purple vest, black ripped jeans, black combat boots, and a yellow necklace, bow, or other accessory. For this character especially, feel free to accentuate your look with makeup—and no, I don't mean clown makeup! A glam smokey eye and red lipstick would be a phenomenal complement to your Joker casual cosplay.

The Joker's Look

- Purple pantsuit or blazer
- Green skirt
- Yellow vest or button-down shirt
- Green bow tie
- Purple gloves
- Black shoes and black heels
- Green or yellow jewelry and accessories

HARLEY QUINN

Another Batman villain is the Joker's erstwhile girlfriend, Harley Quinn. Harley is just as psychotic as the Joker, and to match the theme of his costume, she wears a **red-and-black diamond-patterned jumpsuit with a white collar**, **white wrist cuffs**, **black gloves**, **red flats**, and a **two-toned black-and-red jester's cap**, along with **white face paint**, a **black mask**, and either very **dark red or black lipstick**.

To create a casual cosplay from this look, you can wear a red long-sleeved shirt with black jeans, red shoes, diamond-shaped black-and-red earrings, a black faux-leather jacket, and double ponytails. If you have an article of clothing that features a split-color design with one side black and the other red—for example, a pair of Hot Topic jeans with one pant leg that's black and one that's plaid or solid red—that would be perfect to incorporate into a Harley Quinn look. Similarly, there are shirts, sweaters, and jackets that have a red torso and black sleeves. If you don't have any two-tone clothes, however, you can add the split-color effect to your look by wearing a red top with a black skirt, one red sock and one black sock, and either red or black shoes.

If the red-and-black look isn't something you're interested in, the recent Harley Quinn live-action movie offers an alternative. Alexandra Rita based her casual cosplay on one of the wild outfits Harley wears in the film *Birds of Prey*: a pink bralette, denim shorts with vertical black stripes, neon-orange suspenders, white booties, and a clear jacket with colorful tassels that seem to be made out of streamers and caution tape. She also styled her hair in double ponytails and wore red lipstick, along with a black heart tattooed on her cheek. Alexandra's casual cosplay is a close approximation of the original outfit, as many of the pieces are from the Harley Quinn collection Hot Topic launched in conjunction with the film's release—a pair of distressed denim shorts with vertical black lines, a clear jacket with colorful tassels on the sleeves, a chunky silver necklace with a dog tag, and a Harley Quinn backpack with caution-tape straps. Alexandra added elements that better fit her personal style, though, swapping out the pink bralette for a white shirt and the white booties for white high-top Converse sneakers. She then styled her hair into double ponytails and drew a heart on her cheek. Although this outfit is loud, it may fit some people's everyday style. But if it's not yours, as always, edit at will!

Live-action Harley Quinn's Look

- Pink bralette
- Denim shorts with vertical black stripes
- Neon-orange suspenders
- White booties
- Clear jacket with colorful tassels
- Double ponytails
- Red lipstick

WONDER WOMAN

The last comic book character we'll look at is the DC Comics heroine Wonder Woman. Also known as Princess Diana of Themyscira or Diana Prince, Wonder Woman is an Amazon princess with super strength that she uses to battle villains and save others. She sometimes teams up with other DC superheroes like Batman and Superman, and is most recognizable in her red, white, blue, and gold leotard. The leotard is red on top, with a gold eagle crest across the chest, gold at the waist, and blue with white stars on the bottom. In addition to the leotard, she wears knee-high red boots with white trim, silver wrist cuffs, and a gold headband. To fit this look to your everyday style, you can wear a red crop top, blue shorts with a white star pattern, red high-top Converse sneakers, a gold belt, a gold necklace, a gold headband, and a gold bag.

For my Wonder Woman casual cosplay, I wore a red tube top, a blue circle skirt, a gold belt, gold statement earrings, gold bracelets around both wrists, a gold headpiece, and white booties.

You can also put together a similar outfit using the same concepts but with a skirt that has a star pattern on it. Another way to create a Wonder Woman outfit is by wearing a red dress with a blue blazer, a gold belt, white booties, and a gold headband. If you'd prefer not to wear a dress or a skirt, you can use a sleeveless red top with blue leggings or skinny jeans, a gold belt, gold cuffs, red high-top sneakers, and a gold headband.

Creating casual cosplays for comic-book superheros and villians can be tough, since their attire tends to be extreme—they often wear form-fitting or revealing outfits and accessorize them with capes, armor, or weapons. Don't let that discourage you! You can be the one who inspires others to think more creatively when putting together a superhero—or supervillain—outfit.

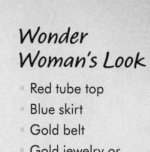

Wonder Woman's Look

- Red tube top
- Blue skirt
- Gold belt
- Gold jewelry or headpiece
- White booties

CHAPTER 8

THROWBACK TV

SpongeBob, Scooby-Doo & More

Whether you grew up with Saturday-morning cartoons or cable TV, there are certain characters that bring you right back to your childhood. Some of my favorite shows growing up were *Scooby-Doo, Where Are You!, The Powerpuff Girls, The Fairly OddParents,* and *SpongeBob SquarePants,* all of which are great choices for those looking to do group casual cosplays.

SCOOBY-DOO, WHERE ARE YOU!

We'll start with the oldest show of the bunch, *Scooby-Doo, Where Are You!*, which debuted in 1969 on CBS and featured a group of teenagers—Fred Jones, Daphne Blake, Velma Dinkley, Norville "Shaggy" Rogers, and Shaggy's dog, Scooby-Doo—who set out to solve mysteries while dressed in the fabulous fashions of the late 1960s and early '70s.

FRED

Fred, the leader, wears a white long-sleeved shirt over a blue collared shirt, cerulean bell-bottom jeans, light brown shoes, and an orange ascot. To put together a Fred-inspired casual cosplay, you can layer a white long-sleeved sweater over a collared denim button-down with blue jeans, brown shoes, and an orange bandanna tied around your neck. If you don't have all the elements of Fred's outfit, you can use what you have on hand.

Cameron Lau (@camerondlau on Instagram) created his Fred casual cosplay by wearing a short-sleeved white collared shirt, dark blue jeans, and brown oxford shoes. Despite not owning an orange scarf or ascot, Cameron improvised by tying an orange ribbon he found in the house to one of the buttons on his shirt to resemble Fred's ascot.

If you're looking for a more feminine version of Fred's outfit, you can wear a white sweater, a bright blue skirt, an orange scarf, and brown booties—but for this character I would suggest wearing blue jeans or pants, as they would reflect his character more and create a better contrast to his female compatriots. Try wearing a white crop top with blue bell-bottom pants, brown heels, and an orange bandanna tied around your neck, and accessorizing with a brown purse. Stick to the white, blue, and orange color scheme and placement and you'll be able to put together a Fred casual cosplay to fit your unique style.

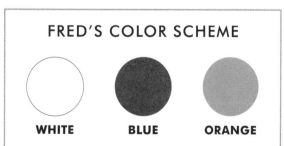

FRED'S COLOR SCHEME

WHITE   BLUE   ORANGE

DAPHNE

Daphne is the most feminine member of the group, and is often portrayed as the damsel who needs to be rescued or protected by Fred and the gang. She wears a long-sleeved violet dress with two lilac stripes at the bottom of the skirt and cuffs over very light pink tights with lavender shoes, a lavender headband, and a lime-green scarf. You can re-create Daphne's outfit by wearing a purple long-sleeved dress, light pink nylons, purple pumps, and a lime-green bandanna or scarf around your neck.

PLUS: lilac or purple headband

But you don't always have to wear a dress to portray Daphne: Erica Lau (left) put together her Daphne casual cosplay with a lilac romper, white sneakers, a lilac headband, and a green scarf. Similarly, you can wear a purple top with a matching purple skirt, purple flats or sneakers, a purple headband, and a green bandanna. Lastly, if you don't want to show your legs, you can pair a purple long-sleeved top with light pink skinny jeans, purple flats, a purple headband, and a green scarf. The most important elements to keep in mind when putting together a Daphne-inspired outfit are her purple dress, purple headband, and green scarf. Other, smaller details, like the pink tights and purple shoes, are helpful but not as essential as the color of the dress and the inclusion of the headband and scarf.

Daphne's Look

- Purple long-sleeved dress or lilac romper
- Pink nylons
- White sneakers or purple pumps
- Lime-green or regular green bandanna or scarf

VELMA

The other female character in the group is Velma, the nerdy one. She's always the one the others turn to decipher clues or offer insight. This egghead persona is reflected throughout her character design: she wears a long-sleeved orange turtleneck, a dark orange pleated skirt, orange socks, dark orange shoes, and black square-framed glasses.

You can re-create this look by wearing the same articles of clothing she does (all the items are available on Amazon), but there are alternative ways to create a Velma casual cosplay. Tara Lau styled her Velma-inspired look with an orange mock turtleneck sweater, brown shorts, white crew socks, black strappy sandals, and black-framed glasses, all of which she already owned. She also put her hair up to make it look like Velma's short bob.

Another version of a Velma casual cosplay would be a bright orange shirt, a darker orange skirt, bright orange crew socks, and either dark orange or black flats. If you don't have an orange top or skirt, you can wear an orange dress and accessorize with darker orange jewelry, bag, or belt. Lastly, if you don't want to wear a skirt, shorts, or a dress, you can go with a long-sleeved orange turtleneck top, a pair of burnt-orange denim pants, orange socks, black slip-on sneakers, black-framed glasses, and an orange beret. If you wear this outfit with another person dressed in Scooby-Doo casual cosplay, the orange color scheme will make it easy for fans to recognize which character you're playing.

Velma's Look

- Long-sleeved orange turtleneck
- Dark orange pleated skirt or brown shorts
- Orange socks
- Dark orange shoes
- Black square-framed glasses
- White crew socks

SHAGGY

Of all the main characters—aside from Scooby-Doo himself—Shaggy has the easiest outfit to re-create. He's a tall, skinny teenager with unkempt hair that goes down to the nape of his neck. He wears a baggy green shirt, loose-fitting brown pants, and black shoes. Although it isn't necessary, having a shaggy hairstyle does help to finish off the look.

You can, however, wear a Shaggy-inspired casual cosplay with any length of hair, regardless of gender. Hali Simcoe put together a great Shaggy cosplay with a black tank top worn under a buttoned-up army-green denim jacket and brown bell-bottom pants from Free People. She even made herself a sandwich as the ultimate prop.

If you don't own a pair of brown bell-bottoms, you can wear brown or tan skinny jeans instead.

SHAGGY'S COLOR SCHEME

ARMY GREEN

BROWN

BLACK

Finally, Scooby-Doo is a brown Great Dane with a few black spots scattered over his body who wears a turquoise collar with yellow detailing. You can put together a Scooby-Doo-inspired look by wearing a brown knit sweater with brown or black jeans or leggings, brown boots, and a turquoise statement necklace. You can also wear a brown dress with a black cardigan, black shoes, and a turquoise necklace or scarf. Remember, even if your outfit is a little obscure on its own, once you're out with your fellow casual cosplayers, your character will really shine through.

POWERPUFF GIRLS

Another set of characters that are best portrayed in a group are the Powerpuff Girls, three sisters created in a lab by a scientist who accidently gives them superpowers. Their names are Blossom, Bubbles, and Buttercup, and each has a different hair, eye, and primary dress color. The leader, Blossom, has strawberry-blond or orange hair that she wears in a ponytail, pink eyes, a pink dress, white tights, black shoes, a black belt around her waist, and a large red bow on top of her head. Bubbles has bright blond hair that she wears in double ponytails, light blue eyes, a light blue dress, white tights, black shoes, and a black belt. Buttercup has short black hair with bangs, green eyes, a green dress, white tights, black shoes, and a black belt. All three girls wear the same style of dress, just in different colors. You and your friends can purchase the same dress in different colors, or you can each add your own personalities and style into your outfits and still come together to represent the Powerpuff Girls.

BLOSSOM

To create a Blossom casual cosplay, you can wear a pink dress, white tights, black flats, a black belt, and a red bow in your hair. If you want to get more creative, though, you could wear a white tank top under a pink blazer and skirt set with white crew socks, black flats, and a red scrunchie.

Erica Lau styled her Blossom casual cosplay by wearing a short-sleeved pink shirt with ruffled shoulders, a two-tone pink skirt, a black belt, and a pink bow in her hair. If you don't have a pink top, you can wear a white shirt with a pink pleated skirt, white knee-high socks, black flats, and a pink or red bow. Similarly, if you don't have a pink skirt, you can wear a black top with white shorts, a pink jacket or other outerwear, and a red or pink bow. Lastly, if you prefer pants for your Blossom casual cosplay, you can wear a dark pink tank top layered over a white short-sleeved mock-neck crop top, pink denim pants, black shoes, and a red bow in your hair. If you don't have a pair of pink pants, you can wear a pink shirt, sweatshirt, or hoodie with black pants or leggings, white crew socks, black shoes, and a red or pink headband or other hair accessory. As long as your outfit includes black, white, pink, and a touch of red, you'll have a suitable Blossom casual cosplay.

Blossom's Look

- Pink dress or skirt suit
- White tights or crew socks
- Black flats
- Black belt
- Red bow or scrunchie

BUBBLES

Bubbles is the girliest member of the group, and always wears light blue. You can put together a Bubbles casual cosplay in the same way you would a Blossom casual cosplay, with a blue dress, a black belt, white tights, and black shoes.

Aside from color, the only difference is the hairstyle. Instead of a single ponytail, divide your hair in two and put it in double ponytails. As an alternative to a blue dress for Bubbles, you can wear a blue top with a black miniskirt, white knee-high socks, and black flats. Since Bubbles's color is blue, you can also just wear a blue top with blue jeans, a black belt, and black shoes.

You can also get creative and put together an outfit you wouldn't normally wear but that's still cute enough to pass as everyday attire. Abby Marrin created her Bubbles casual cosplay using a light blue short-sleeved top worn under light-blue-and-white-striped overalls. She then added a black belt around her waist, white crew socks, and black loafers, and put her hair up to complete her look. One last example of a Bubbles-inspired look is a light blue tank top layered over a long-sleeved white top, a black miniskirt, white crew socks, and black shoes. However you choose to style it, make sure that you stick to the blue, black, and white color scheme.

Bubbles's Look

- Blue dress or jumpsuit
- Black belt
- White tights or knee-high socks
- Black shoes

BUTTERCUP

The third Powerpuff Girl, Buttercup, is the toughest of the bunch. For this character, you can wear either a girly outfit like those for Blossom and Bubbles or something a little more edgy. Buttercup's color scheme is green, black, and white, with a little more emphasis on the black than is found in her sisters' color schemes.

As with the other two Powerpuff Girls, you can create a Buttercup casual cosplay using a green dress, a black belt, white tights, and black shoes. You can also wear a black mock-neck long-sleeved shirt, a plaid pleated skirt, white tube socks, and black combat boots to bring out the edgier side of the character. You can even do a mix of the girly-and-edgy style by wearing a green summer dress, a black faux-leather jacket, white ruffled socks, and black combat boots. Tara Lau put together her Buttercup casual cosplay with a long-sleeved green top, dark green shorts, a black belt, and a black headband. This all-green ensemble may be a bit too out of the ordinary on its own, but it fits in perfectly with the other two Powerpuff Girls. If you'd like an alternative to the green shorts, black shorts would also work. Furthermore, if you're trying to avoid wearing a green top and a green bottom, you can pair a green long-sleeved top with ripped black denim jeans, green socks, and black combat boots or high-top Converse sneakers.

Any way you style your Buttercup, Bubbles, or Blossom casual cosplay, it's sure to look amazing when the trio comes together!

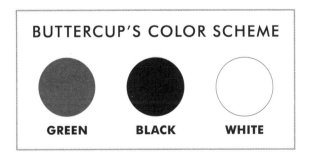

BUTTERCUP'S COLOR SCHEME

GREEN **BLACK** **WHITE**

SpongeBob SquarePants

Another childhood favorite of many Millennials and Gen Zers like me is *SpongeBob SquarePants*, a show about a square yellow sponge who lives in a pineapple under the sea and has a pet snail, works at a fast-food restaurant, and enjoys blowing bubbles and catching jellyfish during his free time. It may sound odd to the uninitiated, but if you ever watch the show, you'll find yourself having a surprisingly good time. Although there are a handful of regular characters, the two we're going to talk about are best-friend protagonists SpongeBob and Patrick.

PATRICK STAR

SpongeBob's closest friend, Patrick Star, is a pink starfish who wears only a pair of green shorts with a purple flower print. Despite the limited color scheme, there are still many ways you can put together a Patrick-inspired look.

One way is to wear a pink tank top, a green circle skirt, and purple accessories.

Another ensemble that would make for a good Patrick casual cosplay is a pink dress accessorized with a green belt, a purple necklace, and a green handbag. For my Patrick-inspired look, I wore a pink, green, and white two-piece set from Lilly Pulitzer that I accessorized with star earrings to represent the shape of the character. I took a few liberties with the color placement but still got my idea across when standing next to Abby in her SpongeBob outfit. A final Patrick casual cosplay might consist of a pink shirt with green shorts, a purple belt, nude sandals, starfish-shaped earrings, and a pink hair accessory.

Patrick Star's Look

- Pink tank top or dress with green belt
- Green circle skirt
- Purple accessories

If you want to take that extra step, you can even cut pieces of purple felt into the shape of the flowers on Patrick's shorts and sew them onto your skirt. When adding details like that to my outfits, I prefer to sew them on loosely—that way I can just cut the thread later to remove them from my clothing without damage or difficulty. If you wish to alter an article of clothing that you don't plan to wear again, you can also paint on the flower pattern.

SPONGEBOB

SpongeBob, as I mentioned earlier, is a square yellow sponge who sports business-casual duds: a white collared shirt with a red tie, tan shorts, white crew socks, and black shoes. Men can put together a SpongeBob casual cosplay by wearing a short-sleeved white button-down with a red bow tie, tan shorts, white socks, and black shoes. The white button-down and the tan cargo shorts in the photo can be purchased from Amazon and Quicksilver, respectively.

For a more feminine SpongeBob look, you can wear a white buttoned shirt tucked into a tan skirt with a red bow tie, white socks, and black flats. An alternative to the white button-down might be a yellow top, worn with a tan skirt, white socks, black flats, and a red headband. Abby Marrin put together a great SpongeBob casual cosplay with a yellow dress from Brooks Brothers, white tube socks, black loafers, and a red ribbon in her hair.

Not only is this dress perfect for SpongeBob because of the color but it also has a subtle windowpane pattern that adds that square detail. As a fun addition, Abby also wore pineapple earrings to represent SpongeBob's unique home.

SpongeBob's Look

- White collared shirt or yellow top
- Red tie
- Tan shorts or skirt
- White crew socks
- Black shoes

The Fairly OddParents

The last throwback cartoon we'll look at is *The Fairly OddParents*, which aired on Nickelodeon and chronicled the adventures of a young boy who obtains fairy godparents who have the ability to grant him wishes—as long as they stay within certain guidelines and follow magic rules.

WANDA

All of the main characters' color schemes and outfits are very easy to re-create. Wanda, for example, is a pink-haired fairy who wears a yellow short-sleeved shirt, a small yellow crown, black pants, and black shoes. You can put together a Wanda casual cosplay by wearing a yellow short-sleeved shirt, a pair of black pants or leggings, and black shoes—as long as you have pink hair.

If you don't have pink hair, you would need to add a touch of pink to your look to represent Wanda's signature hair color. Abby Marrin styled her Wanda casual cosplay by wearing a long-sleeved yellow sweater, black overalls, black loafers, and a pink beret.

She also accessorized with large star-shaped earrings and a wand to further accentuate the idea that she was dressed as Wanda. You could also wear a yellow or gold star-shaped crossbody bag or handbag as an alternative to carrying around a wand.

Wanda's Look

- Yellow shirt
- Black pants or leggings
- Black shoes
- Pink hair accessory
- PLUS: yellow or gold bag

Cosmo

Wanda's husband, Cosmo, is a green-haired fairy who wears a white button-down with a black tie, black pants, and black shoes. Like Wanda, he also has wings and a small crown that floats right above his head. Since incorporating wings and fairy crowns would verge on full costuming, Cosmo casual cosplays are best based on his neon-green, black, and white color scheme.

Men can wear a white button-down, black pants, and black shoes, but switch out the black tie for a green one to represent Cosmo's green hair. Ali N. styled his Cosmo casual cosplay in a similar way by wearing a white long-sleeved button-down shirt, black tie, black pants, and a green beanie to evoke the character's hair color. Actress Esther Lane put together a more feminine Cosmo casual cosplay using a plain white crop top worn under a green tweed jacket with a black faux-leather miniskirt and green and gold jewelry. Another example of a Cosmo-inspired outfit would be a white button-down tucked into black skinny jeans with black flats, a green beret or hair bow, and a gold star-shaped crossbody bag.

COSMO'S COLOR SCHEME

BLACK   **NEON GREEN**   **WHITE**

PHOTO CREDITS

By page number:

14: Tara Lau

15: Tatum Blinn

16: Abby Marrin

17: Krystal Everdeen

18: Krystal Everdeen

19: Erica Lau

20: Abby Marrin

21: Esther Lane

22: Hannah K.

23: April C.

26: Marina Ansaldo

27: Curstie Marie

28: April C.

29: April C.

30: Hali Simcoe

31 (top): Krystal Everdeen

31 (bottom): Abby Marrin

32: Tara Lau

33 (left): Abby Marrin & Tara Lau

33 (right): Krystal Everdeen

34 (left): Erica Lau

34 (right): Abby Marrin

35: Abby Marrin

36: Tara Lau & Erica Lau

37: Curstie Marie

38: Kirsten Lopez & Daniel Rubio

39: Marina Ansaldo

42 (top and bottom): Erica Lau

43 (top): Abby Marrin

43 (bottom): Kirsten Lopez & Daniel Rubio

44 (top): Ali N.

44 (bottom): Kirsten Lopez & Daniel Rubio

45: Karen and Long

46 (left): Erica Lau

46 (right): Hali Simcoe

47: Hali Simcoe

48: Tatum Blinn

49: Tara Lau

50: Krystal Everdeen

51: Marina Ansaldo

52: Jake B.

53: Jake B. & Abby Marrin

54: Tara Lau

55: Krystal Everdeen

56 (left): Krystal Everdeen

56 (right): Curstie Marie

57: Alexandra Rita

60: Tara Lau

61: Krystal Everdeen

63: Erica Lau

64: Sasha C.

65: Erica Lau

66 (top): Erica Lau

66 (bottom): Skyler Talley

67: Krystal Everdeen

68: Hali Simcoe

69: Erica Lau

70: Krystal Everdeen

71 (top): Krystal Everdeen

71 (bottom): Skyler Talley

72: Tara Lau & Abby Marrin

73 (top): Tara Lau

73 (bottom): Kristina Guliasi

74 (top): Kristina Guliasi

74 (bottom): Abby Marrin

75: Erica Lau

76: Krystal Everdeen

77 (top): Hali Simcoe

77 (bottom): Erica Lau, Krystal Everdeen, Tara Lau, Hali Simcoe, Abby Marrin

78: Hannah K.

79: Maegan R.

82: Krystal Everdeen

83 (top): Erica Lau

83 (bottom): Erica Lau & Krystal Everdeen

84: Hali Simcoe

85: Hannah K.

86: Erica Lau

87: Erica Lau

88: Erica Lau & Abby Marrin

89: Abby Marrin

90 (top and bottom): Erica Lau

91: Tara Lau

92: Hali Simcoe

96: Krystal Everdeen

97: Jake B.

98: Alexandra Rita

99: Abby Marrin

101: April C.

102: Hali Simcoe

104: Abby Marrin

105: Alexandra Rita

108: April C.

109: Skyler Talley

110: Krystal Everdeen

112: Curstie Marie

113: Skyler Talley

114: Tara Lau

116: Tara Lau

117: Tara Lau

118: Alexandra Rita

120: Krystal Everdeen

125: Cameron Lau

126: Erica Lau & Tara Lau

127: Tara Lau

128: Hali Simcoe

129: Tara Lau, Erica Lau, Hali Simcoe, Cameron Lau

131: Erica Lau

132: Abby Marrin

133 (top): Tara Lau

133 (bottom): Tara Lau, Erica Lau, Abby Marrin

135: Abby Marrin & Krystal Everdeen

136 (top): Krystal Everdeen

136 (bottom): Abby Marrin

137: Abby Marrin

139: Abby Marrin

140 (top): Ali N.

140 (bottom): Esther Lane

AFTERWORD
Join the Casual Cosplay Community

If you find joy in creating and wearing casual cosplays, you should share your awesome outfits with others who love it, too! There is a wonderful community on Instagram filled with creative and supportive casual cosplayers. Just search for #casualcosplay or #disneybound to find new people and accounts, and use those same hashtags when you share your looks so that others can find you. As I said, I started my own journey by following a handful of Disneybounders—and since most of us have annual passes to Disneyland, we eventually met in person to celebrate together. It's a great way to make new online friends, or even friends in real life (as long as you're safe about it!).

Another way to meet fellow casual cosplay fans is by attending events like Dapper Day at Disneyland, Wondercon, and Comic Con. There are also events that occur across the country year-round, so do some research to find out what may be happening near you. And, of course, you can wear your casual cosplay to the theme park anytime, and I guarantee you'll spot plenty of others in character-inspired outfits, too.

Lastly, if you'd like to share your casual cosplays with me directly, tag me on Instagram @krystaleverdeen in your posts and stories. I would love to see them! And if you want more ideas or inspiration for putting together outfits based on any of the characters discussed in this book—or even ones we didn't cover—you can follow any of the models featured in this book, as most of them share fantastic casual cosplays regularly. You can also follow me on YouTube, TikTok, or on my website, KrystalEverdeen.com, for more outfit ideas. I hope you have a blast—and I can't wait to see all the styles you have in store!

ACKNOWLEDGMENTS

I would like to give the greatest thanks to my amazing husband, Michael. I would not have had the opportunities and experiences I've had if it weren't for you. From taking on full financial responsibility for the both of us so I could pursue my dreams to gifting me with the Disneyland annual pass that would change my life and put me on the path I am on today, thank you for your endless support. I love you so much.

I would also like to thank each and every incredible person featured in this book. I am so grateful for the fact that you believed in me, and I am thrilled to have such creative, kind, and wonderful people be a part of this project. A special thank-you to my dear friends Tara, Erica, Hali, and Abby for swooping in to save the day when I needed it most. If not for your thoughtfulness and generosity in putting together last-minute, at-home photo shoots and modeling dozens of outfits, this book may not have been possible. You're the best friends I could ever ask for.

Last but not least, I would like to thank my family, my team, and the fandom friends I have made all over the world through social media. Thank you for welcoming me, encouraging me, following me, and being a part of this magical community.

About the Author

Krystal Everdeen is a fashion influencer with both feet planted firmly in fan culture, particularly all things Disney. She covers travel, beauty, lifestyle, crochet, and gaming. She graduated from Cal State Fullerton with a degree in communications, entertainment, and tourism. Follow her at @KrystalEverdeen on Instagram, TikTok, and YouTube, or find her at KrystalEverdeen.com.